MARY L. BRO

MARY &
A-HALF

ME MYSELF & I

outskirts
press

FOR DIRECTIONS AND IDEAS

TITLE: Writing from life AUTHOR: Albert, Susan

FOR HISTORY OF ERA

TITLE: The Century for young people
AUTHOR: Armstrong, Jennifer, 1961
REVISED AND UPDATED: Peter Jennings and Todd Brewster

SCRIPTURE SUPPORT

Holy Bible Concordance
King James Version
The World Publishing Company
Cleveland and New York

IN MEMORY OF
BEATRICE DYE AND RAY JONES

Looking back over my life, the time spent with the two of you, truly outweighs any bad times I have ever had. The love you gave me, the patience that you both showed toward me, sacrifices, words of wisdom, encouragements, talks, time, protection, discipline, prayers and complete exception of me as me. All the things a child needs. I am also thankful, that you two lived to see me be in a place of life that was good before your deaths. And that is not to say, we did not have many of happy days, that was good! However, without you I lost my way, yet what you taught me was still in me, therefore I have returned to your teachings and I know that the two of you are glowing with pride and joy, in Heaven. I miss your beautiful smiles that would say you were pleased even in some of my mischievousness you would have a look of disappointment but I could feel your forgiveness. I have so many great memories in my heart, that I can pull from with a smile and sadden many times just because you two are not here, but of courses that's being me a little bit selfish, because I know where you two are and one day, I will join you and we are going to shout all over God's kingdom.

TABLE OF CONTENTS

PREFACE

EVERY LIFE HAS a purpose. Most of us live our lives just wondering what our purpose is, but many searches diligently, to find their purpose. Some never find, some question if they have founded and others know they have founded.

For me to understand with my whole heart of my purpose, I must know the answers to my many questions. Why "GOD" gave me life? Why he gave me free will to make choices? Why he chooses the mother he chooses for me? Why he placed certain people in my path during my life journey? Why he would allow me much joy and much pain? Why must I be one of many to reveal myself to the world, to be appreciated, admired, criticized and dissected all at the same time? However, for me, writing about my life, may just be my purpose coming thru with the life, in which I have lived is a must for me. Now, I know the answers to my questions. This will be revealed as you read my book. Telling on me and others has set my soul free, cleansed my heart of harbored hurts and resentments. Coming to term with clarity of the hurt I caused myself, the hurt that I caused others and the hurt others caused me. In sharing my life with you, the readers, my hope is that you understand we all have been through something. I encourage you to look at yourself with honest eyes, accept your role then forgive yourself. Then get out of living in the rearview mirror of the pain others caused you and forgive them too. I thank "GOD" every day for ever mountain that I have had to climb. I thank him for every valley that I was lost in. I thank him for protecting me in seen and unseen dangers. I thank him for keeping my mind. I thank him for chosen me. I am thankful for this opportunity to share my life story, the good the bad and the ugly.

With one purpose in mind, to fulfill my purpose, that is to share my strength, my gained wisdom, in the hope of helping someone else understand their pathway to define yourself even if you never know your true purpose.

Introduction

I STARTED WRITING my book of my life in March 2007. I wrote faithfully every day until February 2008, I was living in Cincinnati, Ohio at the time. Life showed up in threw me a curve ball so I had to move back to Murphy, North Carolina where I was raised. I stopped writing but the thought of this book was always on my mind to finish someday someway. I stay in Murphy until March 2011 without writing one word. I moved back to Cincinnati in March 2011. I began my new preparation in March 2014 by purchasing a new computer and pulling out all I had written, revising and gathering thought. By September I began to type and to write again. Writing has been bitter sweet, to re-live the pain and to remember the joy. At times I would be laughing, crying, smiling, gotten angry and even sadden all over again, memories, but it was still a must to carry on. My story, my life has something in it that will have you the reader feeling the same emotions, this I am sure. You make have experienced some of my life story directly or indirectly. Maybe it will help you to do something or stop something. Maybe there will be some clarity that will allow freedom and forgiveness. Maybe some increased patients. Maybe anew channel of strength, whatever this book may do for you. But most of all I hope that it will increase your faith in God if you know him and if you do not know God get to know him.

In this book you will read about a child that lived as a child, a child that was full of love, yet mischievous and at times mistreated. I was misunderstood by many, but one lady in particular understood me so well that she used to say to me "you are my Mary in a half." A child that was full of so much laughter, joy and pain. Pain, because one I was "that" misunderstood, being black hated by my country, my skin being too dark for some in my own community, sibling rivalry, child molested, treated badly by adults that did not have the heart to see me as "just" a child, " a little girl. About a teenager that was young and dumb, that did teenager things, that was not so good, bad even and ugly just me being me.

You will learn about a young woman that thrived to serve God, community, family and friends. All was well. However, I was not able to stay grounded. Not because I was doing too much or not enough, I was being abused by my husband, beaten, cheated on, falsely accused, broken down and eventual being robbed of my spirituality for what I had endured for twelve years. Then the pain of a failed marriage, the broken promise of "till death do us part, better or worse", the pain of my children not being raise in a two-parent home.

Now, being a single mother with two small children battling to stay on track, on my own accord leaving God out; not following his roadmap for me. No, crystal ball to show me what laid ahead. Trying to handle my new situations then the death of my best friend in life my mother happened. Then the death of my stepfather, also I lost my best buddy my niece Tiny (Mary Earnest Moreland) all within a two years period. Before their deaths, I had already experienced the loss of two sisters and a nephew big tony (Tony Moreland), he was shot three times in Atlanta, his murder was never solved. In 2003 I lost a brother and my friend his wife in 2004. Not knowing at the time, but I have since learned in rehabilitation that all of that hidden pain, my environment, and me being me, lead me to a eleven year drug addiction and a fourteen months drug program, seven months inside and seven months on the outside, that was very strict and intense and I needed all of it. I was like a wild animal it took all of that, to turn me around and find a new way to live. I had forgot how to live. And yes, I will talk more in-depth about the program and share some of my many experiences in the drug world.

My life not that it is different from anyone else, we all have been thru something, we just handle our situations differently. My thoughts on life pains is, "must Jesus bare the cross along and all this world go free? No, there is a cross for everyone and there is a cross for me". (2nd Corinthians 4:7-10) I will also be talking in-depth of my personal relationships with many. My mother's life, and my stepfather's life and our relationship of pure love. My two children that I carried, which was born in, the eighty's what I call the "eighty's curse first", however the eighties babies and after "yaw" call the "Millennials" and my stepson. My personal relationship with each of my mother's children and talk some about my father's children. My childhood friends that, we have shared a real love and bond that has lasted all our lives.

My relationships with others and what I have learned from those encounters that ours paths cross. Also, let me say this my book is the truth, my truth, what I remember and how I remember it starting at the age of three. I know some may remember what I say differently, but that's alright, this is my story and I am sticking to it. But foremost, I will be talking about my relationship with God and how he was always there and never left me. This I know. looking back, I can see clearly on all the things, he has brought me through. There is no other explanation, but God. Even and my drug addiction state of being, God and I would talk, now, understand this I was never confused on rather it was God or a drug induced delusion or hallucination. I am talking about talking, carrying a real conversation. How God's holy spirit would show up at the right time and at the wrong time, which the wrong time was really the right time, I just did not want to hear it at that time, but I would talk to him anyways and of course I will be sharing some of those conversation that the Lord and I had too.

Although; it has taken me a long time to finish, my book due to; life's circumstances kept me on pause. However; I am so thankful; that, this year, 2020 has forward me the opportunity to finish; also, where I am now; in life and to express my personally opinions; of the world's woes.

My Beginning

ECCLESIASTES 6:10

At the time of my, birth my mother had three adult daughter, three sons and a daughter, then I showed up. I was born in 1960. In a small town known as Carrollton Georgia, approximately forty minutes west of Atlanta. The story my mother told me of my birth, was that her water broken late in the night, she said one of my adult sister (Irma Jean) boyfriend was asked to go get the midwife, instead of my sister staying with my mother, she went too. I was born on the sofa at 4:30am before they returned. I can only imagine the pain and the fear she had to have had. After all there were four more small children in the house, she did not scream, she was afraid of wakening them up. I'm assuming her thoughts would had been, would I be alright, would she be alright and of course the era of the 60's. The unrest in America, the discord amongst the different races, uneven opportunities, the energy of radical protest, from flower children, to religion, new philosophy and the civil rights movements. A time of new ideas, the prospects of exploring space and the depth of the sea. Of course, there was much more going on in the sixty, then what I just casually mention. Which meant nothing to me, I just arrived into this new world of light, space and air, however I did not escape, I grew up in the sixty.

I really do not remember much about my first few years in Carrollton. I do remember us living in the housing projects and my mother's sister and her children lived a door or two above us and we would be playing. One day my sister Evon and I was behind the apartments to far down where there was a creek, I fell into the creek, the water was rushing taking me with it. Evon was running down the side of the creek bank trying to get me out of the water. Finally, I got out of the water. I can only remember being wet and mudded, *never* going back down there anymore. Now that I am looking back on that day, I believe my mother had to have been in North Carolina.

Mama had been working for twenty-four years as a housekeeper, for Elmer and Louise Kilgore. She told me that when she started working for them, she was sixteen, Mr. Elmer was twenty-one and Miss Louise was eight-teen. I do not know what the Kilgors did for a living in Carrollton. However, they were owners and operators of an oil company, they purchased in Murphy, North Carolina where they were distributors to local stores, private homes and businesses as well. When the Kilgore moved to North Carolina they took my mother with them. My sibling and I were left in Georgia for several months with our aunt and adult sisters. Again, I can only imagine what that would have been like for her. A new state, town, not knowing anyone but the Kilgors leaving everything behind that she knew, but most of all her children. She soon became very lonely. The Kilgors lived in the white neighborhood of course and most of the black people lived in the black community called Texana and her only outing was with the Kilgors, she knew nobody, but foremost she missed her children. She begins to yearn for us. She explained to the Kilgors, she could not stay; she wanted to go back to Carrollton because she was worried about us and missed us. Beside the new town and among total strangers, my thought is just maybe her instinct was we were not being taking care of as well "remember the creek."

The thoughts of the Kilgore's losing my mother was not an option for them. The Kilgore's founded her rental house and paid some mover to move us and her things to the mountains of Murphy, North Carolina, located approximately fifteen minutes from the Georgia and Tennessee line. One of the movers was Mr. Felix Blackwell, he was the owner of the truck, and he and his family became lifetime friends of ours, whom I will be speaking about in this book. The other mover was Mr. Ray Jones, he befriended my mother and they had a relationship that lasted for twenty-three years, whom we all considered him as our father figure, we called him pops.

We moved to Murphy in April, 1964; I was three years old. Our house was across town, we lived off the main street, down a dirty road to an area that was called the "Holler." The landscape of the Holler was all the house was on the left side of the dirty road except two, one that was red and sit high on a hill midway down, we were told early on by other older children that, "Redhead Blooded Bones" stayed there, so we had a childhood fear of walking pass there. The other house was near the end diagonally across from ours, on the right with one house sitting at the end of the road. Most of the houses were old, made of wood, with tin roofs, and dangerous porches needing repairs.

The Jacksons house was nice inside and out, but the layout was strange to me. When you stepped up on the front porch to go inside, there was the living room and several bedrooms, cannot quite remember the bathroom; although there were other rooms in the kitchen area. To go to the kitchen, you had to go back outside walk down some steps turn to the right and open the door to the kitchen, which holds plenty of sweet memories, of Mrs. Mattie-belle Jackson and her family.

The house we lived in was brick, inside and out. The outside was a plaster of cement spread over a house frame, the porch and steps were cement and the roof were tin. Inside the house the walls were eight-inch bricks and the floor were cement too, but we had a big rug in the living room. The house layout was upon entering into a large living room, making a left was my mother's bedroom and the bathroom, continual straight into a large kitchen and to the right was my brother's room, my sister and I slept in the living room on a sofa-bed that my mother would lay out every night. My memory is that we lived there for a year, the summer in that house surrounded by all those bricks was like being in an oven, even with doors and windows open, with fans blowing was little comfort. And I must say the heat of that summer was nothing compared to the cold of the winter, "those bricks" held tight to the cold of the weather. I remember mama covering the windows with thick plastic, covering the doors with old quilts and placing old towels at the bottom of the doors to help seal out the cold. All the houses were heated by old cast iron wood heater. Against the wall away from the heater, she had a box filled with old newspaper, another box with kindling, small thin chips of wood and a box of coal, with stacks of wood logs. The paper and kindling were the fire starter, the logs of course made the fire hotter, the coal kept the heat going, which was nice and comfortable as long as you kept the heat up with more logs and coal. In the early morning hours, the fire was almost out and it was cold, but mama would start the heater up all over again, by using a long metal rod (poker) poking into the heater until she got a blaze, then adding more wood and coal.

I had a habit of putting a stick into the heater once it would catch on fire, I would twirl the stick in a fast manner enjoying the colors of the flames. One day reasons unknown to me, I decided to do something different with the flames. I handed my sister Evon the burning stick and told her to stick it to the living room curtains, the curtains burst into flames so quickly, we could not put it out pouring glasses of water on the curtains was not helping. We were horrified. Again, God's amazing grace mama came home from work while only the curtains were burning, she put the fire out. She was so afraid and in shock that we would do such a thing. I also remember the licks she put on us, I thought we were on fire; needless to say, I never played the heater stick game again.

I can only remember bits and pieces of our neighbors and our time living there. The Austin family was a father that shared a house with his daughter and her child, which later on the daughter had more girl that grew up with me and we are still friends, however two of the girl are dead now and their mother became one of my adult sister best friend the mother and her father are both gone too.

Then, there was the Powell family that had adult children and grandchildren living together. The house was always busy with company that seem to drink from sun up to sun down and yes, there were plenty of cat fights and cussing. The parents and many of their children are gone now, but of course there is now a new generation of Powell, they are my friends, one I consider one of my oldest and dearest friends (Sharon) and I have family that has co-mangled and had children together.

The Jones's was, John and Sara they were an elder couple, the parents of Ray and his brother John S. Ray lived with his parents, he was their overseer. Ma Jones was crippled, confined to a wheelchair. I can remember papa John being a frail sick little man, light complexion, greenish blue eyes and baldheaded. He died before we moved from the holler.

I can also remember this elder white lady; her name was Miss Corey, a sweet lady that had a lot of cats. I am sure that is why I have such a love for cats. I would play at her house for hours with those cats and she would always give me cookies and milk.

There was another Austin family relate to the other Austin but lived in a different house. Miss Sara lee and her great nephew whom she was raising, (Emmett) they use to called him Little Boy. I still call him that at times. He is truly one of my oldest childhood friends. I can remember other living there but I do not have any memories of them.

At the top of the holler was a small grocery store. The owner was a small build, short white man; I never knew his real name or cannot remember his name. Everybody called him peewee. His wife name was

Edith and they had one son Ricky. I remember them as good people. They had hearts of gold. They gave unselfishly in time of needs, and I believe everyone in the holler had a line of credit at their store. I can remember going to the store many of times with my mother, she would pick up the things she needed and placed them on the counter, Peewee are Edith would tally up the cost, pick up this little gray tin box open it, pull out a small yellow card with my mama name on the card, then write that amount, then one of them would give me something an apple, piece of candy, gum, whatever. I remember saying "mama, see you don't have to work, they give us food," she laugh and said, "no they gave you a treat, they did me a favor, I have no money, but we need to eat, I have to pay for this food when I get pay." I believe it was that day, I understood her sacrifice for us, and that she needed others to help her.

At the time we lived in the holler, the schools were segregate. My three brothers, Jerry, Willie and Ervin had to walk about two or three miles to the school for Blacks in the Texana community. I can only imagine what that would have been like for three little boys walking that far in the cold, and in the rain. I am sure they were mocked and threaten many times. Although, we only lived in the holler for a year or so; that was not yet the end of our lives surrounding the holler.

We moved into a newly built four-unit government project apartment in early spring 1965. My mother actual lived there for twenty-five years. The apartment had electric heat, three bedrooms, bathroom, kitchen, living room, front and back porch, large front yard, small back yard, hills to climb and trees. I can remember the sweet smell of the newest, the excitement of it all, seeing cars passing, people walking up and down the street. The commotion sent my little mind into an adventurous state of shock. Simply because, I knew this was better, paved road, many cars instead of one or two every now and then, seeing faces that I had not seen. While my mother was busy inside unpacking, arranging furniture, hanging curtains, she told me not to go near the road, but to watch for my brother because we live here now.

I did not obey, again just being a curious child. I saw a lady walking down the street, I ran up to her looking back in fear hoping mama would not see me talking to a stranger or being on side of the road. I said hey to the lady, "my name is Mary I am four, my sister name is Evon she is five, my mama name is mama and I think she is six but don't tell her I told you that." She laughed. Then she said I want tell her. "My name is Mrs. Bessie Carter; I am happy to meet such a sweet little girl." Then she went on to tell me about her church and invited me to come and bring my family too. I ran back inside the house to tell my mama, what Mrs. Bessie had said how we could come to her church, she went to the door but she was gone. That was over fifty years ago. Mrs. Bessie went to be with the Lord on her hundredth birthday, March the 4th, 2019 and according to her family, she had told them, she was going to be with the Lord on her birthday. God is so Faithful. She was still going to the same church until a few months before she passed and over the years, we would still laugh about the day we met. I loved Miss Bessie.

Still on post when my brothers came walking down the street, I ran to them saying, "we live here" grabbing at them pulling them into the yard all I can remember is that we were all smiling. There smile was probably bigger than mind since their walk to school was now a five-minute walk.

Joined to our apartment was another three-bedroom apartment, the Cox's lived their Miss Beulah mae, her adult son Charles, they called him petro. Her husband Otis and their two teenage boys Ralph and Eugene, whom they called sweet-pea.

Above us were two, two - bedrooms apartments joined together. My pops and his mother ma Jones moved into one of them, Miss Emma Cline and her father Mr. John lived in the other. I befriended my new neighbors very quickly.

My mother went to work Monday thru Friday from noon until six in the evening for years. Evon and I stayed with ma jones until the boys came home from school or until we started going to school.

However, Evon and I spent a lot of time visiting our neighbors during the day. I built a special relationship with Miss Beluha-mae, I loved her and she me. What sweet memories flood my mind, whenever I think of her. She worked out of her home mending and ironing clothes for white people and worked a half of a day once a week in this lawyer home. I would sit with her for hours during the day watching her work and carrying conversations with her and at times she would just laugh at something I would say. I do not remember what I would say, I can only imagine it had to have been a question or a statement only a child would say.

Then one day she said to me "you are my Mary and a half." I remember looking down at myself, looking for the other half of me; then saying to her, "no, no half just me," she laughed but she called me that often. I asked her why she called me that, she would just laugh. I can remember her and my mother talking about the day we had shared and again she would say "my Mary and a half. I asked my mother why do she call me that, it is just me, my mother told me it was because she thinks you are a very special little girl. When I was with Miss Beulah I felt like a special girl; so, I just got use to her calling me that. When she would finish her job, she would sometime play the piano for me, I would sit alongside of her as she played. I now wish I had asked her to teach me how to play; however, thinking back, she probably already knew, I would not have been able to paid attention long enough. She would let me help her bake cakes and make homemade bread. She would fry potatoes with onions and pick wild greens. We would sit on the front porch together and she had a box of small piece of cloths joining together piece by piece, stich by stich making quilts.

My favorite time of miss Beulah's chores was when she would wash her family clothes. Her washing machine set outside on the back porch. When she thought they were clean, she would piece by piece place the clothing between two long rolling spools, which mashed out the water. The clothes would fall into a big tub of rinsing water, then she would rinse them by hand, then place the clothes back through the rolling spools, falling into her clothe basket, then she would hang them on the clothes line that was in the back yard too. In the meanwhile, I would be playing on the hill, going into the woods picking blackberry and blueberry, sometimes I would past her the wooden pins to hold the clothes on the line. One wash day while I was playing, I looked up and saw the devil leaning with his chest against a tree. I just stood there, watching him and he me. He was ugly. His color was like a fading black; grayish, red eyes, horns on his head, long arms, long fingernails, a tail, and he was laughing at me, then he begins to motion for me to come to him. I took off running to Miss Beulah, I grabbed her from behind holding her tightly and shaken. She got out of my grip, asking me what wrong with me. I could not answer her. I held on to her dress the whole time we were outside, taking servals peaks to see if he was gone. He was not. I stop peaking, when the washing was done, we went inside, I have now turned her dress a lose but, I followed her from room to room. Normally, when my mama would come home, I would run home, but not this day. My mama came over to get me, and then I latched onto her. I can remember them just looking at each other, then Miss Beulah said "Beatrice, I don't know what is wrong with her." She went on to tell her we were outside washing clothes and that I had acted as if I had seen a ghost. I am still not talking. Now it is my mama time, to be followed from room to room, I even sit in the floor outside the bathroom door waiting until she came out. Until she asks "May-re (her Mary) what is wrong with you"?

I told her. She laughs, but she grabed me and gave me a big hug and tell me, that was just your imagination. Of course, she had to explain what imagination is and yes, she said the devil is real but you did not see him. I went along with what she had told me; that's my mama and I needed to hear that "imagination thing" But I never went on that side of the woods anymore. I never played on that side of our joined backyards anymore without a play buddies and I know what I saw.

One day miss Beulah had finished her ironing for one of her clients; she placed her money on the kitchen table and went outside to help the lady get her clothes into car. While she was outside, this man that her husband would get drunk with came into the house, stole her money and left. When she came back inside the money was gone. She asked me about the money, I kept playing, but I told her she put it on the table. I did not know what had happened. Then in a little while this man came back; she opened the door; he came in and then she locked the door; stepped back in front of him and pointed a gun in his face. I jumped up from the front room floor, grab my doll and hide behind the sofa. I heard her telling him he stole her money. He told her he did not do it at first however; she let him know he was a liar and he was the only one that could have done it. Then he, admitted he had taken her money, but her husband was sick and needed a drink, so he went and bought them a drink, he begins to begged her not to kill him. The fear in his voice, I could feel. Then she said, "I will kill you, if you don't go get my money back." His reply was he had spent some of it on the bottle. Then I could hear him giving her back what he had left, then she told him, he had one hour to bring her, her money back or she would come to his house and kill him; he left. I could hear her open the closet door, placing the gun back on the shelf. Then she called out for me, I came from behind the sofa, she looked at me with a smile, hugged me and said, "I am sorry, I did not mean to scare you, but that "son-of-a-bitch better bring my money back". He did. I do not know if it was an hour or not, but I do know it was quick. I have many stories, I could never tell them all, for many reasons, such as I do not remember, I have chosen to forget and something are best left unsaid.

However, the next two stories are stories that I had rather not share, but it needs telling. I was molested twice but I was not penetrated and almost raped once. Like any other day I am at Miss Beulah, she and I are doing our normal things. When her client came to get her clothes, I can remember Miss Beulah needing to go pay something that day. It had to have been a must because she had never asked a client to take her anywhere before and I am sure as I look back at that day, this I know, if she had known or had any idea, that her husband would had bother me, she would not have left me, with her unknowing "monster" or sent me to ma Jones until she returned. At this time, I must have been almost six. Otis told me to go into their bedroom, I did, then he told me to pull off my clothes and get on the bed. I can still remember that feeling of fear of why and what does this mean? Yet, I did it. He did not touch me, he stayed standing up on the floor closed to the bed, and he unbuckled his pants and begins to play roughly with himself, and then all of a sudden there is white slime all over me. He quickly got a wet washcloth told me to clean myself off, put my clothes on and I better not tell Beulah about this, because if I did, she would never let me come over to see her again and If I told my mother about this she would give me a whipping. I never said a word. Then it happens again the same way. I do not remember why she was not in the house, this second time, if she had left are maybe she was not there when I came over. I do not know. Then one day I was playing with some marbles, miss Beulah had step outside taking a plate of food up to ma Jones. I ran to the bedroom, my childish reaction because she was out of the house and this is what would happen, when she was not in the house, that apparently scared the grab out of Otis, he told me to keep playing. My reaction stopped his hidden dirty secret; he knew my reaction would get him busted, he never bothers me again and I have never told anyone about this until now. I did not understand what that was about until later on in life, when I remember this. He was wrong treating a six years old little girl in such a manner. I know now if Miss Beulah had known about this, she would have killed him, and if my mother had known, she would had too, or have him locked up and the keys thrown away.

When Evon or I was sick and did not go to school, my mother would tell miss Beulah and ma Jones; that one or even, sometimes both us were there to check on us. Ma Jones would come to her door with her cow bell ringing it until we would come to the door; that was her way to check on us as well.

This time I had to have been about seven or eight. I had been sickening the night before with a stomach ache; therefore, I did not go to school this particular day. Miss Beulah son Eugene came knocking on the door, I peeked out the window saw it was him, so I opened the door. He first asked me did we have any onions; we did and went to the kitchen to get him one. I gave the onion to him, and then he asked me did I want to play a game with him, of course I wanted to play a game I am feeling better and we did play "real games" such as Chinese Checker, Marbles and they had a Ouija Board.

Yikes! Now, that Ouija brought back a memory; I was once playing with the Ouija just me and that crazy thing started going all over the place, I had no control of that thing, scared the grab out of me and needless to say I never touch that again, but let's get back to where we were. He asked me where was my toys? The toys were in my room, we walked up the hall into my room, and I began to pull toys out of my toy box that was inside the closet. Then there was another knock at the door, I took off running to see who was at the door, sweet pea (Eugene) tried to stop me from opening the door. I snatched from him saying "maybe they want to play too." After peaking out the window to see who is was, I opened the door, it was Ralph. He asked me was sweet pea here, I told him yes, he is in my room, we are fixing (getting ready) to play a game. I asked Ralph did he want to play with us, he just smile at me and said no, but tell sweet pea to come here, I did they left. Within minutes after them leaving, I heard miss Beulah screaming, cussing, rumbling, objects breaking, and then I could hear that the noise was out in the backyard. I ran to our back door to look out, there I saw Ralph and sweet pea fighting and Miss Beulah outside also with a broom beating both of them until they stop. I was terrified. I had no idea what that was all about. I never said a word to my mother about that day. My little girl thinking was, that I caused it, after all sweet pea had told me not to open the door. I did not go over to see miss Beulah for a while after that, thinking she was mad at me; however, she would see me in the front yard playing, we would talk, I soon forgot about it and returned doing what she and I had always done. When I say, I forgot about what had happen I forgot. My memory of that day resurfaced when I was about fifteen years old. I was watching some type of talk show or special new forum about rape or loss of memories due to something traumatic happen. This woman was describing a childhood memory of her when she was raped by her neighbor. Some of the things she was saying were similar to what almost happened to me many years before. Then just like a light switch my mind immediately went to that day. My thoughts were sweet pea was going to rape me, I did not cause the fight between the brothers, after all and Ralph knew what his brother was up to, therefore Ralph had protected me and beat his brother up, because of his evil action. I felt shocked and unease about that memory, but still I never said a word about it until Ralph died, then I told his wife. A funny memory of Ralph was, when he would past gas, he would lift up his right leg, to let it roar; then he would ask me, "Mary where did that rabbit go?"

Our families had stay friends over the years and I just wanted her to know how much I loved Ralph and what he had done for me that day. Eugene had a short marriage to one of my first cousin and they had a daughter together. Miss Beulah oldest son petro lived with one of my best friend mothers for years; all of those Cox's are dead and gone now. I have no hatred for Otis or Eugene, I just feel sorry for any child as myself; having to go through such, however, the peace is for all the little children; that their "Monster" will have to answers to God Almighty.

Now, that I am older, the one thing that I know is Miss Beulah is the first person beside my mother and pops who really knew me. She called me her Mary and a half, I believe because she understood that I was sweetness, the funnies and the smartness little girl ever! Yes, I was busy, curious, contrary, quarrelsome, and even unmanageable at times. That's the half of me to say "I am special" to her, she liked that about me and in my life, these will be the behaviors, that would cause me much pain and yet, the same behaviors, with "God's mercies" protected me on my life journey. The "whole" I am straightforward, plainspoken, devoted, kindhearted, serious, real and most gracious. I know God created me with all I needed to be able to run this life race, even when I made a wrong turn, my destiny had already been preordained.

Being with my pops and his mother (ma Jones) has giving me the most remarkable, happiest memories a child could ever have. My vision of ma Jones was that she was short, heavy set, light skin and had the pretties long gray hair, that Evon and I would brush and comb everyday sometimes two or three times a day. We just liked playing with her hair and she liked for us to play with her hair. Ma jones did not let her being in a wheelchair stop her from moving about in her apartment. She was fast in her chair. The strength and her arms were amazing for me to watch her roll her chair wheel to get where she wanted to be. Evon and I helped cooked and ate breakfast every Sunday morning with ma Jones and pops. Yes, we ate the "normal" breakfast menu at times, but pop liked nontraditional breakfast. He would eat our leftovers. I would laugh at him and call him silly names when he ate leftovers, such as beef liver cooked with onion and gravy, fried fish, rabbit, potatoes cooked with onion, rice, and leftover bean with cornbread. Now, I do the same. He loved his eggs fried, flipped once without busting the yoke. Once in his plate, he would bust the yoke with his fork, yoke running all in his plate, then he would retrieve the yoke with his bread. I ate my eggs like him at his house to be like him, however I liked my eggs scrambled, then it happens I told him, his way was nasty and I wanted mine scrambled. One Sunday morning pops was having his early morning drink of moonshine, we had fried some pork chops drained most of the cooking grease, then separated the chops. Some of the chops were going to be smoother in gravy. Pops added the extra flour, more salt and pepper, and then he stirred it up until it was brown enough to give me the "ok" for me to pour in the water. This time there were two small glasses of liquid on the counter, I did not know one of the glasses had moonshine in it, but I soon found out, my pops screamed out "oh no that's one was my drink." For us that was so funny, we laugh about it and we ate the gravy. Ma Jones loved apple. To eat them she would cut the apple in half, and then rake across one half first, with a spoon until only the peeling and seeds were left, then repeat the other half. Anytime in the day that she needed one of us, she would roll her chair to the door and ring her cow bell, one of us would go to the door to see what she wanted. At night ma Jones would turn her porch light on and off without stopping until we saw the reflection in our apartment, and again one of us would see what she wanted. Looking back on that seems so primitive, however neither one us had a telephone at that time.

Ma jones was a Christian woman, she would tell me bible stories and how great God was, I believed her but I really did not understand it at all, and she knew that because she would say "you'll understand it all by and by." Which, confused me even more, (by and by?) but yes Lord I do understand? Since she could not get to church by being in a wheelchair this man named Harrison Scott would come every Sunday afternoon to have church with her. I use to get so mad when I saw Mr. Scott coming. I would stop playing, then go sit on our porch to pout and if I was with ma Jones when he came, she would always send me home, now I am really mad then. What I did not understand was why she would be screaming out. Why is he screaming? Why are they clapping their hands? How come ma Jones is crying? I could also hear Mr. Scott reading to her and between reading another word, the clapping, the screams, and the crying would start all over again. Whenever he would leave, he would close the door, put his hat on his head, step off the porch, walk up the sidewalk, into the street and turn the curve. I would run straight to ma Jones to hug her, and get her a towel to wipe away her tears. One day I decided I am sick of Mr. Scott coming down here making my ma Jones cry; I am going to get him. The next Sunday comes and Mr. Scott shows up. I sit on our porch until they begin to do their normal screaming, clapping and such, then I left the porch and ran behind ma Jones apartment and gathered up some rocks. I carried the rocks to ma Jones back porch; I did not know my mother was looking at me out of our kitchen window. She called out to me, "May-re what are you doing?'1 My reply nothing. She said, "yes you are doing something come here". I went to her entering thru our back door, she asked me again the same question, I told her, I was sick of Mr. Scott making my ma jones cry every Sunday and that I was going to knock his hat off of his head, with some rock when he leaves today. She laughed and said "May-re no, you cannot throw rock at people, what if you missed the hat and his head; that could hurt him badly. "I do not think I cared." She went on to explain to me, that the screams were really shouts of worships unto the Lord, clapping of the hands and the tears was about joy, just like they do at church. Since ma Jones cannot go to church Mr. Scott brings church to her. Of course, I did not really understand that either, but mama saw it as good; therefore, I accept it as good. Mr. Scott kept coming, ma Jones kept shouting, I kept sitting on the porch, the only thing that was different, I was no longer angry with Mr. Scott and I started saying hello and good bye to him, Mr. Scott is gone too.

Then one day ma Jones got sick, they took her to the hospital and she died. I remember being so sad, we all were and I worried about my pops being all along. I tried to understand the concept of death.

She is heaven now with God, what I was told, no; she wants be back to her home, I cannot see her again, no more cow bell, flashing porch light, brushing her hair, or anymore Sunday morning breakfast.

However, being a child, I did get over it even forgot about her for the most, yet memories of her would flood my mind over the years of my life, Evon and I continue to cook breakfast with pop for years to come.

My pops and I had a relationship that lasted until his death in 1996. I have nothing but fond memories of him. We would sit out in the front yard under a tree, there we would talk, carve on sticks, chew plug tobacco, and he taught me how to open a pocket knife with one hand and pop- it open, that one skill became in handy later on in my life. However; understand this my pops was not a violent man; I never knew of him every having a fight with anyone. I use to love cutting the grass with him, raking leaves, and shoving snow. As a family we would go to the lake to fish, mostly Evon, mama, pop and I, although I would fish too, I mostly played along the river bank and talked with the other fishermen. We would fish at different lakes and rivers, mama liked to fish at a spot called Canny Creek. She always fished with a stick pole. Her spot was where the water was deepest in a corner of the river, where she would sit on a big rock just drop her line with the sinker, fat juice nightcrawlers "worms" and a float to catch brims. In a short time, she would have a half of a bucket filed.

One day while, fishing I must have been about eight or nine a white boy (teenager?) was diving off the bridge and swimming. I noticed him doing it several times, then his last time he never came back up. I waited for a while, then I asked my mama did she see the boy diving off the bridge, she said "yes," then I said to her, "he has been in the water along time." She asked me was I sure, "yes I replied" so pop drove into town to inform the police, no cellphones. The police came, with other emergency agency, they asked me where about did I last seen him dived from, I show them and then they began to get into the water and unload the boats. While in the boats they threw off these big chains with big hooks attached into the water, as the boats moved slowly, then they hooked him. When they brought him up out of the water, hooks were in his side, his body was blue and a piece of wood was on his head. The wood was a split piece of railroad plank with a large nail spike. One of the spikes were in his head. Witnessing that bother me for a long time, my mind kept seeing that over and over again, sharing that with my mama about my feeling and she would comfort me with words. I had also forgotten about this too, until I begin thinking back to my childhood memories to write this book and then I felt the same feelings all over again. However, now that I am grown, I can deal with the memory of that sight, yet my heart hurt because of the pain his family must have felt, that his young life ended that day.

As a family, we went on many of picnic; we would ride to the Great Smokey Mountains to Cherokee North Carolina to visit the Indians reservation to watch the Indians dance. When we would go to the Smokey Mountains my mother would prepare the night before making sandwiches, green beans, potatoes salad and homemade rolls but she would fry the chicken and make the macaroni and cheese the next morning. On this one particular trip, while they were packing the car, I am running around on the sidewalk and stomp my big toe, pulling off half my toenail, mama cleaned and wrapped my wound, now we are on our way, stopping at a store, for me some flip flops. Upon arriving at the Smokies, we stop at a Scenic site area, which had plenty of other people there.

Then all of a sudden there was a mama bear and two cubs, the mama bear standing upright on her back legs getting food out of the large trash can. Again, I was about seven, my nephew Victor (wootch) was probably around three, he thought the cubs were puppies. He walked toward them trying to whistle, wiggling his little fingers and saying "come mere (here) little puppy." Then the mama bear jumped down from the dumpster to retrieve her cubs, me and my wounded toe took off running, I did not bother to open the car door, I just jumped into the unrolled window and watched from the car as my sister grabbed her son and the bears went back into the woods. All I know, I was afraid and my toe was not on my mine. Another favorite past time of ours were going to watch the community baseball or softball teams play ball, community cook-outs, visiting friends and so much more.

MARY & A-HALF

Now, these outing were mostly fun as a community but sometimes there would be drama or trauma. We all know how we are as human beings. Sometimes someone starts some mess, maybe they did not like the umpire call, just maybe someone from another team said something inappropriate, to a opposite team member or someone tried to finish a personal issue at a time for fun. Drama. On one of the communities cook-outs that was supposed to be fun for everyone went to hell for me and yes, it started out as fun, all of us children were playing, the adults were socializing, the men pitching horseshoes, a couple of older men playing checker, the women are busy setting the table and cooking the meat. However, what happened to me, has traumatize me, to the point that I cannot eat anything, that has not been completely cooked done. When enough meat was ready it was time to feed the children first. The mamas and the other women are calling the children to wash their hands and get in a single file line to eat. The set-up was someone gave us a plate and a spoon, then someone put ours requested vegetables on ours plates, alone with ours chips and bun choice, I wanted a hotdog. The grill had all the done meat, on the far left, the half-done was in the middle and the raw to the far right. It was all good until I got to the grill, this lady looked at me so meanly, I asked for a hotdog, she gave it to me but flopped it in my plate, then I pointed to the piece of chicken I wanted, she gave me the piece, she wanted to give me, she took my piece of chicken from the middle of the grill. While in line I could see and hear how it was going, for those in front of me. Walking back to the table, I was feeling bad, that she did not treat me like the other children. Placing my plate on the table and sitting down, the blood from the half-done chicken, had gotten all over my food. I just sit there and washed the other children eat. At this very moment, I must admit, feeling that pain all over again, as I fight back my tears. Not, necessary of what she did, but why she did it, I did not know that lady and she did not know me, I do not remember being around her at that age. Maybe she did not like me because of old ladies' gossip, maybe the way I played or maybe I seems spoiled coming up to my mama often. I have no idea.

However, that goes back to learn how to forgive other and I do. When I'm down south if I see her, I speak, carry on conversation. I have wonder if she remembers, I will never ask, but I will say this, "little children grow up and they do remember."

Let's get back to my pops. Pops did drink a lot, I did not know at the time, that his drinking was a sickness, called alcoholic, for me he was just drunk on any particular day. One day he was cutting the grass while drunk, he hit a bottle that was near the outside water hydric. I was making mud pies, I had no shoes on, and I went to get more water for my mud pies and stepped on the glass and cut my foot. I had to go to the hospital to have nine stiches in my foot. My mother was furious with him. I did not understand why, for me it was just an accident, for her it was that he was drunk and if he had not been drunk, he would had stop to pick up the glass.

There is other community called Marble, which had a slaughter pin, mostly mama, Evon and I would ride with pop there to get fresh hog chitterlings. They would clean them and we would eat them. One day for whatever the reason was pop and I went along to the slaughter pin, when we returned again, my mama was furious with him, I did not understand why, we went, we are back, so what is the problem?

The problem was he was drunk.

For many of years pops was a bootlegger and drinker; I rode with him a many of times to pick up the "Shine." We drove so far back in the mountains, where there was only a couple of old wood houses, no power and we ran out of paved roads; just dirt and rocks. The mountain men were white, long hair and long beards, their accent was country beyond country, then there were the hound dogs, cats, goats and the pretty's garden, I had ever seen. Now, that is a lot, because the old farmers in Texana had nice gardens. My pop and the mountain men would handle their business with talk and sampling of the product. Then they would load the cargo in the trunk of the car, give us fresh vegetable from their garden, and give me fresh apple picked from the tree and one or two dollars. They would shake hands and make plans for the next trip. Before we had left my pop had been promising me that I could drive until we hit the paved road again, this was the day. He got in the driver's seat, I got in his lap and I drove down the mountain, what a great day for me until we got back home. My mama was furious with him and I did not understand why, so I asked her. "Why are you mad we went to see the mountain men, I played with the animals, they gave me money, apple, they sent you fresh vegetable and pop let me drive the car down the mountain, oops! Then she looked at me and said "and I thank God that you are home". My little brain went all over the world then. Then she said "Ray is drunk". You could have driven off the mountain and died, he could have wrecked on the highway with his drunken ass and if the police had stopped him, they would have taken you both to jail. I understood that and I never would ride with my pop anymore if he had been drinking and I started hiding his keys. Then it happens, the police caught him driving drunk, he went to jail, lost his license but they gave him privilege license to drive to work and back home. He did eventually get his license back and he did not drive drunk anymore. When pop was at our house, he would sit in his favorite chair that was against the wall headed into the kitchen and he always kept on his cap. I got a thrill walking into the kitchen pulling off his cap and popping him on his baldhead. Then I would reach around the side of the kitchen door pull off his cap and pop his head again, until he would get mad, then I would stop. He never spanked me or my sibling, that I can recall, although he was going to spank me one day for something, I do not remember why, but just maybe because I kept popping his head. Anyways, I remember him jumping up, pulled off his belt and his pants felt down, the waist part was around his ankle. I stood there and just laugh and laugh and laugh, he reached down, pulled his pants back up and put his belt back on. My pop came to our house ever morning during the week, on his way to work to eat whatever was left over from our super the night before. I thought he was crazy, to eat beans, greens, cornbread, whatever for breakfast and I would laugh at him about that, but guess what now I find myself doing that very same thing. When pop would be reading the paper, he would hold it way out in front of him and turn the paper at different angle, I would tease him about that because, I thought he was playing like he could not see, now I know, I do the same now. My pop would say to me on a bright sunny day that it is going to rain because his joints were beginning to hurt, again I would just laugh and say "right pop" but now I can predict the rain because my joints will begin to hurt. My pop favorite saying to me was "pretty is pretty does". He would always say that to me, when I would brag on something I was wearing or if I had got in some kind of trouble. I did not understand what he was telling me for a longtime, and then one day it dawned on me. It really does not matter how pretty you are if you are doing things that are not right your ugly. Not to say I stop being ugly, it was some words of wisdom that I heard, cherish and today live by.

The next best thing, he could have ever told me was how to fight a pack of girls. I had told him that some older girls had been bulling me, calling me name and had been threating to beat me up. I was afraid. He told me, "this is what you do if they bother you again, if you can pick up a stick do so, if not just quickly grab the meanest girl first, then you start hitting her as quickly and as hard as you can without letting up and I promise you, you want have to worry about the others because they are not goanna want none." For whatever the reasons were those girls did not bother me anymore, but a few years, the opportunity arose to prove, his advice to be true, you will read about that further on in the book.

The older I got, I guess between eleven and twelve during the summer my pop would come to our house every day for his lunch and I would have him a big glass of ice water and something to eat. Pop's job was in Marble, working at the lumber yard. One day he did not come home for lunch, he came home late that evening with his hand all wrapped up, with a metal plate under his thumb. I tripped out "oh pops what happen." His hand had slipped from the wood going through the saw and cut the tip of his thumb off at his knuckle. I immediately became his nurse. Every other day I would change his bandages until it was healed. I learned early on that the body knew, what belonged where although he did not have but just a little bit of a thumb, his thumbnail would still grow and I kept it clipped for him for years.

Another time my pop got sick, his nose started to bleed, he and I tried pinching his nose, holding his head back, but it would not stop. Blood all in the sink, on the floor and blooded towels, I want it to call for help, he said no just wait, but I did not wait. I called His friend Mr. James Bush, screaming telling Mr. Bush my pops is bleeding to death, Mr. Bush came right over taking pop to the hospital, which was just on time, pop was hemorrhaging, he stay in the hospital for two are three days. Pops told me that they packed his nose, but that did not stop the bleeding, then he say they put some type of instrument in his nose that burned broken vessels to stop the bleeding, this one time my disobedient saved my pop's life.

I loved playing nurse taking care of pop, I remember one time his Conjunctiva (bottom inside red membrane of eyes) in both eyes had so much inflammation in them that his Conjunctiva was swollen so much they were on the outside. Every day I would put his eye drops in until he was healed. I was not turned off by any gore, I was always willing to help, and for me I want it to be a Doctor when I grew up. However, I did not stay focus on my dream and that's okay God has something else for me to do.

Our pops were good to all of us; he would buy food for the house, help with all holiday expenses, school trips, supplies and whatever else we needed. However, one day my bully brother Willie and my sweet brother Jerry got into a sibling fight in their bedroom. They were teenage boys. I am guessing they would have been around fourteen and sixteen. They were going hard at each other. I am all in the way trying to help Jerry, throwing in my hits and kicks against Willie. My mother had bought Jerry a guitar, the guitar was on the bed, and Willie threw Jerry on the bed and broke the guitar. Jerry had just started his lessons, with Deacon Hall. Now his guitar is broken, he is crying, I am crying, the situation did not affect Willie at all. Jerry became in a rage that, I had never seen in him, Willie either. The fight got even more insane. My pops heard all the confusion and came down, to break up the fight. Pops had his hand full, the more he pulled them apart, the more they would lock up. Then pops got angry and came a little more agitate and begin to remind them of when Beatrice gets home. That all he needed to say was the magic word "Beatrice." My mother was furious at them fighting, I do not know what their punishment was, but I do not recall them physically fighting again, and she had the guitar fixed.

I am not sure when my pops brother uncle John S moved from his dwelling place in Hayesville North Carolina about twenty- two miles from Murphy to move in with my pops in his two-bedroom apartment. I believe it was not long after ma Jones passed away. I am not sure of the time frame, but not long after, Uncle John S moved in, he was introduced to a lady. She was the sister and aunt to a family friends and she became my Aunt Lillian. She had been living in Cincinnati for years, came down to attend their family reunion in Bryson City North Carolina. My uncle John S met her they felled in love, married in 1969.

The three of them lived in the same apartment maybe a few years. Then they moved into the cox's three-bedroom apartment, a bedroom each. The three was truly the real three musketeers" one for one and one for all." They lived their life their way. They worked until they did not have to work anymore. They had they're on space and place. They shared their bills, food, moonshine, love for one another, and yes, they would tickle me when they would get into their little disagreements. My aunt Lillian and I had closeness like Miss Beulah and I. Aunt Lillian always had the most food; her kitchen pantry was stocked like a mini grocery store, as well as her refrigerator, freezer, and cabinets. She was talented. She would knit covering for furniture, make dolls, jewelry and she made my prom dress. Aunt Lillian had a "green thumb" whatever she planted would grow. Alongside of the apartment from the front, side and back was the loveliest flowers, that would grow as high as the apartment windows my eyes had never seen such beauty. She also grew tomatoes and watermelon and at that time I thought watermelon was only red inside, but some of Aunt Lillian watermelon was yellow inside and so sweet. Aunt Lillian had a little Pekinese dog name Tiny that she treated like a child. Yes, Tiny went to the veterinarian, she knitted sweater, bought collars with fake stones, Tiny had her on bed and toys. Tiny favorite snack was frozen hotdogs cut into cubes. With this new media craze of animal's lover, it seems new but it is not, this dog had it all.

Summertime was always, the greatest time with Aunt Lillian her, daughters, grandchildren and great grandchildren would come down from Cincinnati to visit and again I would go with them on road trips, play with the other children and search and find four leaves clover for hours and yes, I would always find the most. Being with Aunt Lillian was a happy time and place for me; however, I did get in trouble with her and Uncle John S once. Aunt Lillian had a crystal cubic piggy bank with pennies in it, I did not care about the money I want it the crystal cubic. So, I took it. The next day they asked me about it and I denied it but they knew. Uncle John S was most upset, so finally I confessed and begin to cry and told them I was sorry, please forgive me, do not tell my mama and I will go get the crystal cubic and bring it back. I returned it still crying, they hugged me and said it's all over, they won't tell and I better not ever do that again and I did not at least from them. After I became a teenager and could drive, I would drive Aunt Lillian to place she needed to go sometimes. After, a while Uncle John S was unable to drive far distances, I started driving Uncle John S into the back mountains to the moonshiner, he did not bootleg, this was his private stash. With all my driving there, I never learned my way to the moonshiner, he had to direct me every time.

Aunt Lillian died first, Uncle John S and Pops continual living in their apartment for many years after her death. later on, Uncle John S only daughter lived in, Asheville North Carolina came and took him to live with her, she had concerns of him aging. Uncle John S lived many years in Asheville, he was the last to past of the three "Musketeers" he was in his ninety. Although they are gone, their love and my love live on and I thank God for allowing them to be a part of my life.

My pops did go to church, although he continuously to drank for years. I sung in the church youth choir, and he loved to hear me sing. I must admit he was probably the only one who did. He would always go to different churches which; we as a church were invited to, just to hear me sing in the youth choir. After I became grown and sung in the adult choir he still came, and would tell me how great we sounded and how it gave him joy to hear my voice. I sounded alright with the rest of the choir carrying my voice, because I cannot sing really, but it was music to my pop's ears. Later on, my pops stopped drinking "praise God" and he joined the church. I knew when he was happy in the service because he would begin to cry, and tears of cleansing, joy, gratitude and the filling of the Lord's Holy Spirit on him was obvious to me.

Pops did have one daughter, Sarah Ruth; she was in the age range of my three older sisters. She was married, her husband Claude was a soldier in the Unite State Army and they had five children. Their age range was like ours, Debbie, Claude Jr, Sherry, Bonnie and Lagail. They were always traveling and at one-point Sarah Ruth and the children lived in Murphy and the children attended school with us. I do not know why; however, I believe it had something to do with her husband's military duties, he did return to get them. And over the years they returned many times to see pops. As years past pop got older and they had to remove one of his legs, and his health was not good. Sarah Ruth came to Murphy and put him in the nursing home for a while, and then she returned taking him to Florida to live with her. When he passed away in 1996, Sarah Ruth had him brought back to his hometown, Hayesville, North Carolina for him to be buried. Sarah Ruth had asked Evon to get in touch with me, her reason was, she told Evon was because she knew how much her daddy loved me and that he loved me more than her(which was only because I was three his new little girl) she want me to speak at his funeral. I did speak. I remember telling all the people that were there what a great pop, he was and the love, we had for each other.

Then I broke the sadness by telling one of my favorite stories he had told me. Pops whole name was Ray C Walter Earnest Lee Jones, (C is for Charles) I remember my mama saying to him about his name was because pops mama had promised every white person in Hayesville that she would name her baby after them. Whatever, he told me while on one of his moonshine runs, he had some truck trouble. Unable to get the truck started, he began to walk in the rain and cold for miles until he came upon this one lonely house in the mountains. He said he walked up on the porch and knock on the door, then a woman answers saying "who is it" he replied Ray C Walter Earnest Lee Jones and she replied "I don't have room for all of you "son-of- Bitches" keep moving." Pop said he had to walk some more miles before he came to another lonely house on the mountain, when he knocked on that door, he said his name was Ray Jones, they let him in and helped him on his way. What a story of many and I am not sure if this story was real or not my pops said it and I believe him. Truly a good man regardless of any short coming, he may have had. All I do is remember the great moments, we shared and look to the promise that I will see him again.

(John 8: 7) He that is without sin, let him or her cast the first stone. We all have sinned and felt short of Gods Glory. I said that just to really say this, I do not know why my pops drank the way he did for years. I can only speculate and my speculating comes from, what I was taught; about my own drug addiction, while in rehabilitation. Although, there may be other reasons, the counselors focused, on three main reasons. One being, environment, two, hidden hurts and pains and three, some of us are just, inclined to having additive behaviors. His environment was living in a small rural town in the 1920's, with the population of Blacks were probably less than one percent. A place and time when you were "White you were really right." Jobs were probably far in between and everybody had to do whatever they could to survive; moonshiners made the illegal liquor and the bootleggers sold it, sampled it and got addict to it; that was the biggest part of their environment. Secondly, hidden hurts and pains will keep you stuck. Staying in that pain, he self-medicated (stay drunk) to covers up the pain. He too, had a failed marriage, he had another brother that was killed by some white men; he also had friends and family members killed in the wars but; I'm sure he had more pain than that and the third reason, being inclined to having additive behaviors, I cannot speak of that for him, only for myself. Now, with that being said, I'm sure you the reader maybe thinking; his life style may have affected me in my on addiction. I doubt it. Sure, I was around him drinking, however, that is only a small part of my total environmental places and spaces. My pops had been an alcoholic and alcoholic thinking is non-rationale; therefore, he was unaware of how his behaviors affected those around him and if he knew, he was unable to control himself. I know he did not mean to do me any harm.

BEATRICE

PROVERBS 31:10 WHO CAN FIND A VIRTUOUS
WOMAN? FOR HER PRICE IS FAR ABOVE RUBIES.

SHE WAS CALLED mama by her children, sometimes B-Dye jokingly,
her grandchildren called her Big Mama, grandmamma or granny and
called Aunt B by her nieces and nephews. Her friends called her B. Dye,

pops called her Beatrice, our friends called her Miss B. and some of our friends called her miss. B. Dye. What is in a name? The many names she was called represented who she was to each individual that choose, to call her what she meant to them personally or what their level of knowing her. She was a humble woman, sweet, strong, wise and very serious. She was not a cursing woman, she did not need to, she was a master in sitting anyone straight quickly and you knew it. She had a lovely smile, a low tone to her voice, her laughter was soft and rarely a stressed face. I have never saw her drunk, but she would have a sociable drink on rare occasions. She always bought these little seven-ounce pony Miller's beer that she kept under her bed, placing some in the refrigerator to cool for some of her friends, when they would come to the house. As we got older, we would steal them. She also kept switches twisted together, in the kitchen pantry, on the shelf for us just in case. She was faithful to the church, where the church went, we went. On special occasion when we would eat at the church, she was always asked to make the rolls and macaroni with cheese, for the church dinners. We were made to go to Sunday school every Sunday. In like some lyric in a Stevie Wonder song, we would keep some of our Sunday school money to spend at Mr. Author's neighborhood store. She was a school mom attended many school meeting and baked cookies at times for the school event. We were poor compared to some of our friends and other neighborhood children. Many having a two-parent home with both parents working, so they had more I could see. However, we never missed a meal, our power was never off, we were never homeless, we never missed a holiday celebration or anything we needed. I have looked back and wonder how she did it, but God blessing her for her righteousness. I am sure she had to have had many sleepless nights, on whatever the task, at hand would be accomplish; but her faith and the people in her life was, there to help her, this I am sure.

Beatrice-Truitt-Brown-Dye was born September 6th 1920 to Jenny-Mae Truitt. Jenny-Mae married, a Will Brown of Roopville, Georgia approximately twelve miles south of Carrollton, Georgia. Mama, the baby was two years old, her oldest brother, Harvey and Katharine. Harvey was killed on a railroad track when he was about nine. Aunt Kat had seven children, Albert was already born when she married Eddie Ackey, out of that union, they had Ed-Lou, James, Annie-Mae, Dianne, Patrice-Ann and Bobby all still living but Bobby (Frog) and Aunt Kat died in October 2009 at the age of ninety-two.

Mama was born humble, that was her natural sprit, being sweet was her destiny. Her wisdom, strengths and serious attitude, was learned by living the life; of her era, on live terms. Making mistakes alone the way, however; she too had many sad and uncertain days, yet, she was happy and at peace, for years when her life was over. I can only imagine the wonders she, saw living in the era she lived in, the apprehensions, she must have felt. When I decided to write about my life, I realized I cannot tell my life without telling her life, it is only because she lived, that I lived and how my molding arrived.

The 1920's were really the decade of when modern society began. The movies, automobiles, airplanes, radios and women are voting. Al Capone and mostly gangster in the North, Ku Klux Klan grew rapid in the South creating fear in the black population and the stock market crashed. She was nine years old when the "Great Depression" was going on. People were struggling to eat, unemployment was at a high the world had ever seen, factories and farms were closing, and she shared with me of those times. She told me that her dad would leave for weeks even at times months to fine work. She loved her daddy. A daddy's girl. She would be over joyed when he would return home, she said they would walk for miles, to reach the river bank to fish all day. She was his "girl boy" meaning she was his sweet girl riding his back like a horse and yet, she would also help him plow their land using a mule flipping the soil of the earth, for their garden and her daddy never ever spank her.

The stories she told me about her mother, my thought was the movie "Mother Dearest." Her mother had mental problems, she was psychotic, neurotic (CRAZY) completely unbalanced and did spend some time in a psyche ward later in her life. Mama told me that, she and her sister had to carry water from a creek until they had water well at their house. Coming from the creek carrying to buckets of water was hard not to spill some, if her buckets were not filled to the rim, she would have to walk back to the creek to get another bucket of water. Sometimes, her mother would just tie her to the bed post and whip her until blood would ooze from her torn skin. She also shared that her mother would get her and her sister ready every Sunday morning to go to church with their grandpa Brown. Early one Sunday morning getting the girls ready for church they thought, she took them to the water well to throw them in, she said they were running and screaming when their grandpa showed up. Telling him she was trying to throw them in the water well. The girl stayed with their grandparent from that point on unless their daddy was at home. and as they became older, they did return to their parents' home. My mother never told me about any good times with her mother nor did she ever say anything against her either, she only said what had happened to her.

My mother lived to see thirteen presidents starting with Herbert Hoover. However, for her the greatest of all was Franklin Delano Roosevelt. Restoring hope into the people with his "New Deal Program," and she had trust in this great leader of this time. Again, times were unstable dictators snatching other countries, Adolf Hither of Germany taking Europe, Italy takes Ethiopia, Japan attach China, France bombs Britain and the Japanese attach American soil, by bombing Pearl Harbor, fierce times.

In relations with those times, her life was unstable too. Her mother was still mean to her, and one day while out she met Fate Dye. A charmer, funny, smooth talker a working man, and she was mitten, a whirlwind courtship, she married him within six months at the age of sixteen. For her this was also away to escape her mother, however within six months of marriage, her mother's house felt like a dream house. Her husband was a drunk(alcoholic}, cheater, and abusive in every way possible. She gave birth to their first child Fannie Mae May 1937 their second child Lula Mae was born November 1939 and their last child Irma Jean was born October 1941. My mother told me that she knew her husband had been untrue but she did not say at first how she knew or why she stays with him. Then she said people were talking saying her husband was cheating on her with her best friend, she could not believe that. She stated to me "she was my friend", she ("FRIEND") would take mama and the girls to the movies, bought things for the girls and she would tell mama things fate was doing, this cannot be true." Blinded by the light.

Now, this story gets creep. My mother told me that she had four dollars, she put two of them in her top dresser drawer and went to the store to get some bread and milk with the other two. As she was approaching the store a lady called out, she looked back, then the lady said to her come here a minute. Not knowing the woman, she kept walking, then the woman yelled out "you have been worrying".

Mama said she thoughts, I have been worrying but maybe it was showing on my face, how else this stranger could know. Then, the lady said gives me two dollars and I will show you why you are worried. Mama told the lady I only have two dollars and I am buying milk and bread with them. Then, the lady said I am not talking about them two, I am talking about the two you hid in your top dresser drawer.

Mama said the hair stood up on the back of her neck and she ran into the store. Upon leaving the store walking by the woman said keep your two dollars; you will see yourself in two days. Mama said two days later she had left work early, she had something to do, and then she saw her husband and her best friend in the car together. When her friend saw her, she laid down in the car. Later on, that night she confronted her husband about her seeing them, he denied it. She said she kept jugging at him until he said "yes, I have been courting her for seven years and I am going to court her for seven more. Mama no; it is time for you to have her. When she left her husband, Irma Jean was nine years old and she had been working for the Kilgore's for thirteen years. They founded her in the girls a small house and paid for her divorce. Mama made two vows to herself, one never lives with another and never be treat, the way her husband did, meaning fighting and cheating and she kept those vows.

The first time I met Fate Dye I was about twelve, we were at a cousin's house visiting in Carrollton. I will never forget his remarks of claiming fault. He said "Beatrice was a jewel of a wife and person", mistreating and losing her was the biggest mistake he had ever made, wishing he could turn back the hands of time." Fate did marry the other woman and I can remember over the years when we would visit family in Carrollton, we would go with my sisters to see their dad and his wife. My mother had a forgiving heart, she forgave them. When he died my mama and two of their daughter, Irma Jean and Lula Mae and their children attended the funeral.

Between 1946 and 1952 World War Two had ended, America comes into another good era, Harry Truman was the President and in mama's opinion, Truman was just alright. The first electronic computer was built, penicillin was discovered, people were buying houses, streets were fairly safe, and it was good times. However, for Blacks, the possibility for equality was still a decade away. Jackie Robinson breaks the "color" barrier in professional sports and Truman integrated the Armed Forces.

And, yes fear still lingered in people minds about the possibility of another World War, that could end the world with Nuclear Weapons. Not only did the United States have such weapons, Russia and China had them too.

With all that being said life was good for her in the girls. For her, no husband to treat her badly and she was grown living alone with her girls and no "Mama Dearest" to take advanced of her unjustly. She was happy and free at last, still working for the Kilgore's by day and working at a small cafe in the evenings as a cook and dishwasher. Not glamorous by no means but sufficed enough to provide. She was able to go out, meet new people and live her life her way.

It was at this time she met a man named Ralph McCoy. It is the early

1950's, Dwight Eisenhower was President, suburb living, supermarkets, chain stores, malls and American Bandstand was the show to watch. Eisenhower. she liked but felt he was timid and could had are should had did more. This was the start of the civil rights movements, with the Montgomery, Alabama bus boycott and the Supreme Court's ruling what was unconstitutional and it was up to the Federal Government to see that the states, cities and counties abided. Eisenhower, was dealing with peaceful and unpeaceful marches.

The courtship of my mama and Ralph lasted for five years, she bored him three sons. Their first son Jerry born, 1954; then Willie Ralph born, 1956 and Ervin born, 1958. She told me that she was six months pregnant with Ervin when they departed ways and Ralph moved to Youngtown, Ohio. She did not say much about him accept he too drank and would not keep a job.

Again, when we would visit Carrollton, mama would take the boys to see Ralph's family. They knew their daddy's sister and a few cousins. Later in life after Willie was grown, he also moved to Youngtown and lived with his daddy for a while, then they both returned to lived back in Carrollton. I really do not know when Jerry came in contact with his daddy again, but it was long before Ervin had met him for the first time. Ervin, was grown and there were pictures of them together, I have no idea where the pictures are now. I, too met Ralph when I was a young woman and the boys had many features of their dad.

While at his apartment in Carrollton, he spoke mostly about being remorseful toward the boys; not being the man nor the father he should had been and he was proud and happy to have finally seen Ervin.

Not able to recall how long after they reunited, that Ralph died, I know they went to his funeral along with mama.

Not long after Ervin was born, she started a weekend job at a night club (juke joint) as a cook and dishwasher and that is where she met, Rufus Thomas. (Not the famous singer) She never said what kind of work he did, but he did work and kept money. I learned later in live thru his family and people that knew him, he was mostly a hustler. He too drank, bootlegged and played the guitar at the same club and was a womanizer. They had to girls together my sister Evon born, 1959 and me, 1960. I do not remember much about him. My only memory of him, I was about six or seven, we had gone to Carrollton and she took Evon and me to see him. I looked a lot like him. I remember him having on overall, me sitting on his lap and him giving me some money. That is the last time I saw him, he died when I was eight, mama attended the funeral, not sure why she did not take Evon and I.

At the time when mama was married to Fate Dye, Rufus had a wife they had six children, their name are Betty, Sara Mae, Linda Jean, Peggy, Lorrain and Charles Rufus. His wife died when the children were young, he met a lady named Miss Tina, she had two young girls of her own, their name are Jo Ann and Kalinin, they raised the children together and Miss Tina bored him two girls, Sapphire and Vicki. Yes, I have or had seventeen brothers and sister knew them all and loved them all. Of them, the only one's left is Lorrain, Sapphire, and Jo Ann. A funny story, mama told me about my dad, was one day while in her back yard, she was washing out by hand some shitty cloth diapers of Evon's in a wash pan. She said he came up talking crazy, wanting to argue and making threats. She said she took a stack of those shitty diapers and started hitting him all over, he ran and never tried to bother her again. That was one of her vow.

It is clear to me, the fascination of the men in her life wanting her. She was tall, slim, pretty and had hips. She was somewhat submissive toward them, strong, independent, did not drink nor smoke. I can only speculate as to why she would have dealt with them. Maybe her thinking was being a divorced woman with children, most men did not want an already made family. Also, the area which she lived; men were few. As a woman, she had a woman desire for companionship. I think for the most part, she accepted her circumstances out of some form of necessity, the old cliche "sometimes you have to do what you have to do to get what you need."

My mama never wanted eight children. She told me that birth

MARY & A-HALF

control pills were not readily available, they were not free at that time; only women with, the means to purchase them had them. She stated to me, "if I could have got them, I would had, pilled myself to death". Unable to afford them was unfortunate to her. I responded to her by saying, "God knew what he was doing, he wanted us here and he wanted you to be our mother." She responded with a proud smile that I would say that and then she said, "I am sure you are right." She had a gift for mothering. I had many friends and my cousins telling me, they wished my mother was their mother. I was the type of child, that only a mother with her grace, patience and the strength she had, to handle and love me. She loved us all equally, yet having the natural ability to manage each sibling individual based on our personality.

B. Dye had strong opinions of many things, but her heart was heavy laden with the troubles of the world. I must say, as much as I miss her, I am glad she is not here to see this world.

In the early 1960's John Fitzgerald Kennedy was president, she loved him. She thought he was cute now, but more than that she thought, he had the heart to enforce the rights for all the people. When Kennedy came into office, there were many troubles on our own home front, however the world around us seemed to be more pressing for his concern. The Bay of Pigs invasion, deteriorating of Southeast Asia, the possibility of Russia given Cuba, Nuclear Missiles to attach the United States and the building of the Berlin wall. In June, 1963 he changed the inequality of Blacks from a legal issue to a moral issue, by proposing the Civil Rights Act. During this time Blacks, wanting equality were being met with hatred, water holes and attacked by police dogs. President Kennedy was assassinating in Dallas Texas in November, 1963, five months after his proposal.

Vice President Lyndon B. Johnson became President in signed the Civil Rights Act in July, 1964, thirteen months after Kennedy's death. I can recall my mama having a picture in a nice frame hanging on our wall, of President Kennedy, Martin Luther King and Bobby Kennedy. I asked her one day who were they, I knew the face of Dr. King and

I remember his death; because it was on the television news, for days and my mother was so sad, but who were the other two? She told me who they were and that they were all killed, shot down just because they were for the same rights, for black people and making peace in the world. Being a child, it is understandable why I could not comprehend that statement as reasonable. So, before I could ask her to explained, she said, "I do not understand either." Yes, she understood it was about hatred and not wanting changes, but what she knew was, I would not have understood it, if she had told me the "why." Upon finishing Kennedy's term, Johnson ran for the presidency and won serving as President until 1969. Mama did not like Johnson, she believed he had something to do with Kennedy's death and she thought he was racist. Even though he, had helped Black American, by signing the Civil Rights Act of 1964.

Signing the Civil Rights Act of 1964 made Johnson a "Civil Rights Hero." For the first time making democracy real to black people. Wiping out Jim Crow, blacks could now use public accommodations, government accountable for equal employment and all federally funded programs. Coming off the skirt of the Civil Rights Act was the Voting Rights Act, the 1965 Social Security Act Amendments and the 1968 Fair Housing Act. Johnson was a big man from the big state of Texas and had a big domineering personality, which cause many to believe his attitude escalated the Vietnam War. His popularity demises quick over that war and many believed his Acts were only being signed due to the outbreaks of riots in the homeland. The Harlem riot in 1964, Watt of Los Angeles in 1965 and over a hundred in April, 1968 after the assassination of Dr. King. Even though, I did not understand the full scope of the war or the impact of Dr. King's death, I can recall mama unconsciously praying out loud to the Lord about all the young men dying, the pain of their families, who will continue the struggles, asking the Lord to bless. This I remember because, I heard her praying and the words, she would be saying often.

From 1969 to 1974 Richard Nixon was president. Nixon ended

the Vietnam War and improved international relations between Russia and China. Nixon's Secretary of State, Hendry Kissinger negotiated disengagement agreements between Israel and Israel opponents, Egypt and Syria. Nixon's Foreign Policy was great and he ended the Draft. Yet, the Nations were still divided, wars overseas, turbulence in our own cities and the country is in an economy crisis. America shows support to Israel in their war with the Arab, therefore the pipelines are cut off resulting in gas and oil prices went up.

Richard Nixon is the only president to have resigned from office resulting from the Watergate Scandal. Again, B Dye did not care that much about Nixon, however she thought he was an intelligence man, she said she knew he was a crook before the world did. During the Nixon's Era end I was like thirteen, I remember the things that were going on and in school talking about the president going to be impeached. Of course, again my age and my mind frame, I did not understand what this meant and I really did not care.

Upon Nixon resigning from office, Vice President Gerald Ford became president from 1974 until 1977 finishing up Nixon's term. Ford basically acquired Nixon's mess. However, Ford was credited for helping restoring public confidence in government after Nixon's Watergate Scandal. President Ford struggled to work with a Democratic Congress. "How ironic is that, Obama has suffered the same fate working with a Republican Congress." Ford could not convince congress to approve military aid to South Vietnam, which alluded the South to fall to North Vietnam at least that is what history has implied. Ford did reduce tensions with the Soviet Union. Ford lost his race for the presidency in 1977 to Jimmy Carter.

Many believed and including mama that President Ford had tried hard with heart, he held the Nixon' Era as a bad omen for him.

President Carter severed office until 1981. I can remember mama being excited about President Carter, the Peanut Farmer, seeing him as someone that could relate to the real issues of the people. Americans people was grasping for new hope. Carter was honesty and wanted to eliminate government secrecy. His Foreign Affairs reopened the United States relations with China and made gain with efforts for peace in Arab and Israeli conflict, which was damaged late in his term with the crisis in Iran. Again, we are facing the possibility of another cold war with Iran. The American Embassy in Teheran was taken over and held hostage, almost fifteen months. That I can remember from beginning to end and it was frightening. Most Americans were still suffering, the energy crisis, high inflation and unemployment.

Mama loved President Carter, she thought he was strong at heart, weak on arms and too sweet for his position, however she continues to love President Carter.

My mother and I were very closes. Honestly tell her things, of course not everything. Something I would say, she would say "well May-re I would be ashamed." I loved combing her hair, holding her hand, massaging her shoulders and helping her cook. The greatest part of my relationship with my mother beside our love, was that I was always aloud to have my own opinions. Even as a child I could express them, although they did not win often. However, when I became grown, we enjoyed respectfully discussing our disagreements in there were many. There were many times she changed my mind, but it was few times I changed her. One example was the 40th president known as the "Great Communicator" Ronald Reagan, began his Presidency, in 1981 until 1989. She did not like Ronald Reagan. (She loved him as a human being.) She thought he was an actor and was just acting, she thought he was just for the rich "Reaganomics" and simply could not be trusted. All of that may hold some truth. However, I liked President Reagan, he to me was very intelligent and serious with protecting Americans, and he did not play and was unafraid. With congress in legislation, Ronald Reagan stimulate economic growth, curbed inflation, increase employment, cutting taxes decreased government expenditures, restoration of prosperity and peace through strength. Iran also freed the hostage the day after he enter office and like the Nixon scandal, Reagan had the Iran Contra Affair scandal. However, the weight failed on Lieutenant

Colonel Oliver North, that's the dirt of politic, someone have to be, the "fall guy". I remember mama feeling so sorry for the Lieutenant, having to take the fall, I am sure there were a lot more to the story but the Lieutenant was not innocent and Reagan was not either. Reagan strengthens our national defense with his "Star Wars Program," which led to a large deficit. I remember at the time mama and I thought that money should have been spent on earth instead of space. Now, I think Reagan's "Star Wars" was a good investment, we the United States has the best defenses equipment in the world. He negotiated with Soviet leaders a treaty to eliminate intermediate range Nuclear Missiles. In 1987 President Reagan said to Russia General Secretary, Mikhail Gorbachev "Tear down that Wall." In referent to the Berlin wall that separated East and West Germany. Neither, mama or I knew much about the wall, I just remember her fear and her saying, "That fool is going to get us in a war with Russia." My thought was Ronald Reagan is "crazy" yet, I figure he knew what he was doing, and that was Reagan behavior. Also, in 1987 the stock market crashed, known as Black Monday, similar to the 1929 crash just not as devastated. President Reagan Presidency ended in 1989, his Vice President George H Bush ran and won the Presidency.

President Bush served one term from 1989 until 1993. He enters into the office talking about a "new world order," a kinder and gentler nation. To mama, Bush was just another Reagan clone. Bush Presidency the Berlin Wall did fall, he had an anti-drug program, panama overthrow Manuel Nortaga and Iraqi invaded Kuwait, which was inevitable pulled the United States and their Allies into the Persian Gulf War known as "Desert Storm," at least that is what history will record.

This war was very personal in our family and our community Texana, we had six members in that war.

One of my best childhood friend Renee, she had been in the Army, now serving in the National Guards of North Carolina; along with other Guardsmen, when they were sent for duty. Renee's brother-in-law JT

Nicely, Henry Allen, Jewel Jackson, Mack Pickens, the father of Carl Pickens, Cincinnati Bengal's wide receiver, my nephew Victor Lewis Holland(wootch) was in the army, when they were sent for duty. I had been receiving phone calls from wootch at times. One night he called me and I could hear the bombs, airplanes and the fear in the voices in the background. He wanted to tell me he loved us all and that his group was in long deep trenches they had made for shelter and waiting on backup. I told him "do not die, do not be afraid, you fight and I loved him too." I thank God they all made it back home.

Watching the war on the television, the display of high-tech weapons computer-guided missiles, seeing satellites mapping targets for direct hits, it was amazing to watch and for mama it was just unbelievable. In again, the Bush Era yield faltering economy.

The last president mama saw in office was Bill Clinton, she compared him to Kennedy. He is young, smart, good-looking and for the people. Now, if she had lived to see President Obama, she would have loved everything about President Obama and I would have had to spend many days of conversations with her about him. However, knowing my mother, her first concern would be, "they are going to kill him." Then she would have believed "they" will do everything possible to hinder his ideas and not give him his due credit. Well? President Clinton severed his presidency from 1993 until 2001. The Clinton Era, we Americans enjoyed peace, prosperity, low unemployment, budget surplus, declining crime rates, free trade agreement, new technology and a peace accord with Northern Ireland. Clinton's promiscuity scandal, she remarked, "he was a man before he was president and other politicians are doing the same things; just have not got caught." Well?

Thus far I have tried to set up a foundation of who we are or who we were, however those random stories are nowhere near, yet. Since we are in the BEATRICE'S chapter let keep rolling on who my mother was as a woman, friend, mother, lover and "human." As a woman, she was no different than any another woman as far as women issues and concerns are. Her only uniqueness was her own personality of how she views things and how she would handle things. She did it her way.

She had many friends. Now that I am looking back at her friends what I have notice is that they were different as night and day compared to her, yet for her she had the ability to understand and to accept people as they were. Now some of her friends may have had personal reasons not to like some of her other friends, but some just did not understand what she understood. She understood, "that there is so much bad in the best of us and so much good in the worst of us so who has the purity to judge another." My mother met people where they were. Everybody had a chance with her, that does not mean everybody could be her friend but they were not her enemy either. She would say "some people you have to feed with a long handle wooden spoon," other words be kind but keep your distance.

Mama had many friends but her best four friends would have been Mrs. Laverne Nicely, Mrs. Beatrice Bush, Mrs. Emma Cline-Moore, Mrs. Grace Maudlin. These are the women I will share some detail, of their relationship. I will name some of the others, not to say the love was less it was mostly circumstance, they were not part of her normal circle; they were in the same community clubs or church ministries. Mrs. Laverne Nicely, to us she was Miss Veen but to mom just been. They were two peas in a pot. I never seen nor felt any tension between them, although there were times of tension due to something one or the other may have been going through and they would sit at our kitchen table to talk about it and those times were far in between, mostly it was just talk and laughter. I cannot say when their friendship started, she was always there. Miss Vean came down every Saturday morning, for the two of them to go shopping, mostly to the grocery store, window shopping and if on the occasion extra money was available momma would buy clothes, shoes or other items. They loved to go to yard sales and flea markets for fresh fruits, vegetables and anything else they may see. I can recall times when things were needed or maybe mom wanted but could not afford, Miss Vean would show up at the house with it. My mother would cry, thank her and say "you should not have done that," Miss Vean would always say, "you needed it; did you not." Miss Veen husband Melvin family was out of Hayesville, North Carolina, so she attended Fort Hembree Baptist Church in Hayesville most of the time. Our church was Mount Zion Baptist Church and they did go to each other's church on occasion. Her husband just like my pop was an alcoholic and sometimes, she would come and spend the night just to get away from him. It was not out of fear, I remember her saying "I just do not want to be bother with him, listening to his nonsense and I am afraid, I might end up kill him." I do not believe she really meant that. They stayed together until death did, they part. It was not just the ladies hanging out they went out and about as couples with their better half of course they may have seen it as their worst half. (laughing) One of my fondness memory of Miss Veen, was her smile and laughter; of something, I would say and I could see the proudness in her eyes. She could cook too. Miss Veen had a cast iron wood burning stove. This stove was huge. The stove top plates were thick, round with a small cut out for the purpose of lifting up the hot plate with a rod to stir in the hot wood for even heat. The oven part was just as an amazing how she would cook breads, pies and cake inside the oven for a while then remove them out of the oven and place them beneath the oven to another place so the item could brown on the top. Yes, it was a lot but the love and effort were necessary and worth the effort. I use to love seeing them all dressed up for Christmas parties as a child for me their style of clothing, high heels, hairdos and the costume jewelry was so different, yet equally beautiful. They spent time enjoying each other plants, old music and hours of conversation. They had a bond that could not be broken and they were still friends when I became a woman. I was around them quite often and learned much from them, however I recall as a child, I was sent out of the kitchen at times because something was being said I did not need to hear. Miss Veen use to drink milk all the time, she said it cooled her burning ulcer. I remember Miss Vean fanning herself often and she would say, "I am having a hot flash," I recall asking once "what is a hot flash," mom ordered me out of the kitchen, but "oh I know now." My mama had such a balance on discipline; she seemed to know which disciplinary action to take at all times. Rather she chose to spank, punish, just talk and even prayed for us. I did get a spanking once; that she later learned was a lie, her response was, "well it was for the one you should have got; that I missed." My thought was, yes, the things she did not know about. I brought all of that up just to set up this story.

One Saturday afternoon, I must have been around thirteen, mama and Miss Veen had come back from the stores doing their normal routine, putting up supplies, admiring their purchases and talking. I was getting "cute to go somewhere. I laid the comb down on the sink while I clipped another part of my hair. My brother Willie came around the corner and took the comb. I asked for it back several times, he refused and I was furious. I went to the kitchen and told my mama, she took the information lightly and told me to calm down, he will give it back in a moment. In that moment, I had a quick mental breakdown. Less than a minute, I started cursing and saying "you did not hear me, I had the comb first and was still using it, why should I have to wait; he should have to wait." Then, my senses came back. I ran out the door as for as the sidewalk near the road, then I just stopped. I had never talked; that way in front of my mother or her friend before or ever again, the shame in my heart caused me to stop. I turned around looking toward the house to see my mama walking toward me, I just stood there. She casually grabbed my arm and escorted me back into the house to my room and closed the door. I was thinking about the spanking that I would receive at any moment; however, I did not care, for me that would have at least eased the hurt and shame. After a few hours, she returned to my room and asked me was I ready to eat and I was. After I had eating, she began to talk to me about what had happened; she asked me, "Why would you do that?" I explained to her again about the comb and I felt like you did not care enough for me to stand up on my behalf; to make Willie give me back the comb. I did not understand why I needed to wait, "I had it first" and I thought you could not hear my cry because you and Miss Veen was into the new purchases making my situation "nothing." She just stared at me for a while, which seemed like a long time, and then she said "ok I will I give you that one, but you will not get another one." She went on to say, that I must apologize to Miss Veen and I did. She also told me, that she would pay closer attention to avoid another outburst. I apologize to my mother hugged her and it was never talked about again.

Over the years they remained best friend going thru a lot together. Anything that life threw their way, from deaths, children troubles, community issues, good times and bad. Their friendship was like a marriage, till death did they part. They loved each other, they were true, no lies and their secret were their only. Miss Veen lost her battle with cancer in May, 1986 she had been sick for a little while and during her sickness like most friends, my mother was there, I would drive mama to Miss Veen's house every day; so she could help keep Miss Veen clean, see that she ate and to be each other strength during that trying time. Over the years my mama talked about her friend, how she missed her and shared some funny story of her and you could hear the joy in her voice but still see the sadness in her eyes.

Again, I really loved all of my mama's friends, yet I had a very special connection with her friend Beatrice Bush. Now, that I look back on their friendship, I can see why I loved Miss Bush so much, for so many reasons. As I share keep in mind, that the reasons or from a child perspective. I think mainly because her name was the same as my mother and Mrs. Bush physical self was so cute to me, she stood about four feet; eight inches, dark complexion like me and bowlegged. I think a lot of my attraction to her was she and my mother had disagreement just for the sake of disagreements. Been around them, I learned just because you are friends do not mean you will always see eye to eye. I remember hearing them having their little disagreements but never disrespect of the other opinion. Moreover, Mrs. Bush was a little "pit fire" my meaning of the word was she was very opinionated, therefore my mama would checked her often, however Mrs. Bush would keep her opinion and *inform* my mother that she was just to kind, trusting or naive, which none of those reasons was true, they just had differences on how they viewed situation. I believe those differences was the bonds that kept them friends for over thirty years.

They addressed each other as B. Bush and B. Dye. They to spend a lot of time together mostly thru the week days, Mrs. Bush would drop by and they talked often on the telephone. They were in several different community clubs and church business together and Mrs. Bush would always pick up mama, mama did not drive. Mrs. Bush was married her husband name was James Bush and they had two sons, James Junior and Willie Gene, they were both older than my brothers a few years, they were friendly with my brothers but they traveled in different circle. I use to love going over to the Bush's they would pick us up, other times my pop would drive depending on how much he and Mr. Bush planned on drinking. The Bush's did not live in the Texana community they lived across town, they had a nice home and dinner at the Bush's was great, we ate foods that we rarely ate such as steak and trout and chef salad compared to hamburger patties, perch and garden salad, however do not miss understand that statement, I am thankful for what we had, I just loved treat nights at the Bush's.

The years between 1966 and 1969 from my memories, the Texana community baseball team was playing a lot of ball. At that time they played on a field where the high school is, Mr. Bush had his little concession stand selling cokes, peanuts, hotdogs and candy, I worked for my munches by helping Mr. Bush to put drinks in his tin tub he used as an outside cooler and retrieving the homeruns balls from the bushes or long side the river banks. When I was a young girl, I was sick a lot needing to go back and forward to different Doctor in Asheville, North Carolina. It is just another blessing in our lives of friends. Mr. Bush was a chauffeur and he had the skills for driving and the willingness to drive us to many of my Doctor's appointments. Yet, I really must say I was scared half to death of Mr. Bush driving, he always took us in his red stick shift truck, believe me when I say he would put smoking tobacco in his pipe, light it with matches, smothering the flame with his hand, turning the truck wheel and changing the gears all at the same time.

I am not sure when the baseball team subsided, however the community had a softball team that endured well up into the late 1990's or early 2000's. Many times, the two B's rode togeter; we wer at the age now; that we wanted to walk to the ball field with our own friends. One day Mrs. Bush stops by to bring something by, she had not planned on getting out of her car because she was blowing her car horn. Mama friends did that often for one of us to come to the door. They would tell us to relay a message to mama or come to the car to get something they were bring. This particular day I ran straight out the door to the car to ask Mrs. Bush to come inside. Evon had a piece of tape, she had rolled up tightly and was digging in her ear with it as it was a Q-tip. and she lost grip of the tape and we could not get it out. Mrs. Bush got it out and told us not to be put anything else in ours ears every again, we agreed, hugged and thanked her and of course she told mama about it but that was ok.

Mama loved to knit and sew. I can remember her knitting gifts for some of her friends and Miss Bush always had her to mend or hemp some type of garment and cook certain dishes for her and the aroma would be so lovely, many times I would ask what you are cooking, that is something for B. Bush and do not touch it. Both of the Bushes are gone now, Mr. Bush died many years before his wife death. I really did not even come close to sharing the years of our time with them in our lives. Remembering them brings back a simpler time filled with so much peace, joy, love and tenderness to be around them. And yes, I would ask to many question, touch something I should not be touching, doing something I should not be doing, however they would laugh at times are put me in check and I always complied because I always felt their love and I them, often thinking about them.

"Miss Emma Cline," we first met her in the spring of 1965. Again, she and her father Mr. John lived above us in the newly built housing project. Miss Cline and mama also had a friendship; that lasted over thirty years. Looking back on their friendship all I can see them having in common was church community services and the women clubs. These two was as different as night and day. Miss Cline was outspoken about everything, mama usually kept her opinion to herself. In speech Miss Cline was very proper, sophisticated even elegance one may say. Mama was soft-spoken her voice was low but some of her pronunciation was not proper. Miss Cline did not have any children; she had a sister that had a daughter, they came up from Tennessee often to visit. Beside their community functions, their togetherness was mostly standing in the common area of the yard to talk or the occasional times on the side of Miss Cline's apartment lounging in lawn chairs in the shade while sipping on freshly brew ice tea. When I think about them drinking tea, I can recall Miss Cline's fancy matching, rainbow colors glass tea set, with pitcher, glasses and tray. We knew to be very down-low with our behavior if Miss Cline was home, she was what we called "noise," she would tell on us if she saw, heard or heard through the grapevine she would tell, I learned early on not to let Miss Cline know nothing. I know she had our best interest at heart and we all loved and respected her.

I think I was about nine, I wanted a Blackberry Pie. I asked my mama could I go into the woods to get some blackberries. Evon and I walked up this deep embankment directly behind our apartment to the woods; we both had full buckets of blackberries. On ours return to the embankment; I made it off the bank safely placing my bucket on the back porch. Evon was sitting on the bank whining that she was afraid to come down so I went back up the bank to help her get down. Then she decided she did not need my help; she could get down on her own, yet she was still sitting there, I reached out my hand to her saying give me your hand, she made a quick hand motion toward me while saying go away I can get down myself. In my reflexes I jumped back stepping on a lose rock and fell off the bank. After landing in the backyard I jumped up quickly saying it did not hurt and we began to laugh. As I waited for her to come off the bank I started to dust the dirt and grass off of myself, then I noticed blood on my hands and my clothes, then I started to search myself to see where the blood was coming from, then I saw and it was over. I screamed and ran into the back door where my mother was standing in the kitchen, I ran past her thru the living room, out the front door, alongside the apartment, back inside the back door, thru the living room, out the front door, and then I ran to Miss Cline telling her I was dying please call me an ambulance. She asked me what is wrong with you, reaching out to grab me; I took off running again right into my mother's arms. When they saw my leg, my mother held on to me and they held on to each other. I had cut my right leg just below my knee on the outside of my leg from the top part of a broken glass coke bottle. The cut was so deep you could see my bone, not a piece of bone the whole bone, also nerves, artery, veins and muscles you could sit a tea cup inside the cut. Miss Cline called Miss Bush to come take me to the hospital; in the meanwhile, mom wrapped my leg with towel and comforts me. This I will never forget and yes, I was so scared at the hospital, I would not let them help me. They then wrap me in sheets, taping me up, leaving only my leg out stitching it from the inside out.

Mrs. Emma Cline-Moore, she too has pass on and I often think about her, the colorful clothes she wore, the way she could pop chewing gum with every chew, the way she walked, the way she talked and the clothing she wore. I can recall several ladies in the community would call me Emma Cline on occasion and I must admit I did not like it. My thought were I am a young woman in my early twenty begin compared to a woman that's in her late sixty, I thought it was coming from a negative point of view and it may have been, however now I see it as an compliment, she was an lovely lady inside and out.

Mrs. Grace Mauldin, she and Miss Cline were best friends to each other, like Miss Cline she was proper in her speech, sophisticate in her style, nice shape and gorgeous. She came down often to visit Miss Cline, but she did come see my mom on occasions.

From a child point of view, I saw their friendship formed, basically from a mother to another mother.

Yes, they too were in the same community groups and the church, but I think "the tide that bonded" them was us the children. Mrs. Grace was married, she in her husband WT, had four children Michael, (Jermaine Dupri father) Lucy, Ford and Jenny. Jenny is one of my best friends in life and our birthdays or one day apart, I am the oldest and Ford was my first boyfriend, we will talk about that further down in the book.

Once I can remember some trouble arose about some scratches on Michael's little red mustang. Whatever had happened my brother Jerry was blamed for it, Jerry denied it and he was the type of child my mother trusted his words. What I do remember about it, the mothers talking on the phone, they were not angry and the issue was settle.

My brother Willie, the high school football star and Lucy the cheerleader captain it would seem to be a perfect idea to date, however that turn out to be a young mistake decision. Do you remember me saying, I got a whipping once that I did not deserve? Jenny and I had a fight, girl to girl combat, first and last. I had scratched Jenny somebody told that I had cut Jenny, and then somebody called, kept the lie going and my mother, she knew I was capable of doing such. After the whipping, she called Miss Grace to see how Jenny was, Miss Grace was like what, Jenny is fine and yes, Jenny does have a few scratches but no, that's a lie.

What I admire most of their friendship, was no matter what, we had going on between us, they never lost the sight that children will be children. They represent "real women" of yesteryears past. How sad is it that, now mothers support all their children nonsense and grown women cannot control themselves in a manner to talk with one another about their children issues?

I can recall during one of our mother and daughter conversation; when mama said there were other women that she was acquainted with, felt like Miss Grace was "to upped," she never said who; however, the Maudlin' was the "Jones." They owned their home, they had several cars and trucks Mrs. Grace worked, her husband was a truck driver, raced cars and whatever else he made have done to support his families, and they were blessed with the finer things of life. My mother said she never sensed any form or fashion "I am better then you," and again I say my mother may not have had what some of her friends had but what she did have they needed, which was her strength, honesty, encouragement, frankness, understanding and wisdom. The older their children got the more they talked on the phone, in the yard and wherever it may be. As a mother of four and a mother of five young children it would, had to been hard to do much but children. Yet, their friendship was real and lasted for thirty years. Mrs. Grace, sadly passed away in February, 2018 and I will be sharing more about her later on, in my book Mr. Mauldin, passed away in June, 2010.

Mama had so many friends and it has been such an honor for me to look back on their relationships. Also, for the people of our community to remember their names and to tell this new generation, about the women of gold. To have been there, to see their difference personalities' and to show how their friendship affected me. My mother never told me how to put her friends in a particular group or order, I just know Miss Veen was first. However, sharing my life thru her life, there are other women that she shared a bond with that was very special to me also, that I must at least mention their name and a few memories.

Miss Louise Colbert, whom I and some of her grandchildren called her "mama Essie," she was the grandmother of many of my childhood friends and my running partner Renee, whom I will talk about later, in depth. She too was in some of the same community clubs as my mama and of course deeply involved in the church. Miss Louise had eleven grown children, when I was little girl and was raising three of her granddaughter, so yes she and mama had a lot in common; they were good friends, with all that life throw their way they made it and Renee and I was their "thorn in the side." Mama Essie too has passed on.

Mrs. Ella Jackson, whom everybody called "tootsie" even her own children, which was not that uncommon for many of the families in Texana, to call their parent by name. Tootsie and my mother also shared a bond of motherhood, she and her husband, Jackie had eight children and was raising her brother Larry. Larry and my brother Willie were friends and he became my husband, which no one saw coming not even us. However, he is now my ex-husband. Tootsie is the youngest of all the mothers.

She and her husband Jackie were hard working people and provided well for their children. I can recall tootsie being at the house quite often with her children and we played a lot together, however they were younger than us except the oldest two boys were around my age. Again, she and mama were in the same community clubs, however, she attended the Methodist Church across town. As a child she was one of the greats, of community leaders. It was not uncommon to see her with other people children, along with hers' going on nature walks thru the woods, on the river and to the ball park. As I got older, I saw how she fought for our community portions, it did not matter if it was a county program or state funded monies, she would seek it and more times than not get it. She had a way of knowing what was available and informed my mama plenty of times of things she made be eligible for, and there is more, that I will talk about later in the book.

In the beginning of my book, I talked about a few of my mama's friends that did not belong to any clubs and was most definitely different than any other of her friends but none the less of her friends.

One of three that come to my mind is Emmer Colbert; she had one grown daughter and the grandmother of four of my lifelong friends, Doug, Mary, Tony and Melissa. "Emmer was a trip." She lived by herself for the most of my childhood, until she began a longtime relationship with a man from Hayesville, North Carolina and they stay together for years. However, that did not change her; she continual being a strong-willed woman, sweet, funny, loud, vulgar and a drinker but not a drunk. She too was a housekeeper, kept money and always drove a large car. She was always at the baseball and softball games; I do not remember her being at many or if any community picnics. Emmer and my pops were related and drank together on occasion. When she would come to visit, she walked in the door with craziness, saying and doing anything and my mother would just laugh at her, not at what was being said or done, but rather than her boldness of stupid stuff. I remember when I was about nine or ten, as soon as she walked in the door, I am sitting in the floor and Emmer asked me "girl you got any hairs on your pus yet?" I just looked at her, it did not frighten me, because I was already use to her saying and doing crazy things. My mama would speak up and say "Emmer, you should be ashamed and watch your mouth." Emmer, response would be" let me see it." Of course, I did not; however, Emmer said that to me for years. Then she would go on into the kitchen sit down at the table and visit for a while, she did not come often but when she did, she was always the same. That was just who she was and she stayed true to her personality no matter where she was. I think the base of their friendship was more then, here being my pops family member, but their differences. They were friends for years just maybe Emmer wildest was what by mother needed at times to be free of her normal life, for just a short abnormal moment of the un- normal fun.

I can recall Melissa, the youngest grandchild, we all called her "Baby" having had some medical problems with her ears; did affect her hearing and speech. Baby could not say Emmer, she said "Member" and we pick it up and called Emmer, "Member" too. Emmer too has passed on. I must say at this very moment, I can feel my eyes beginning to fill up with tears just thinking about "Member's goodness." I am not thinking about her incorrectness but only her correctness, how she loved me as one of her on grandchildren and yes, she said "crazy stuff" to them too, but always giving to us her time, words of the wise, money, candy, rides, whatever, whenever, and she would cuss us out too. Her favorite saying was, "don't do what, I do, do what, I said to do." If she saw us, in the wrong just hoped you were far enough, that she could not get a hold of your ears. She too has passed on; may you rest in peace "Member". I loved you.

Mrs. Annie Hubbard was another assorted friend of my mother; she too was a relative of my pops Mrs. Hubbard and her husband Frank lived in Hayesville, North Carolina. My memory of them was mostly around the age of about twelve. Mrs. Annie loved to drink too and would say some wild things. However, she was unaware that, I was always close enough to overhear; just being nosy until mama would catch me ease dropping and run me away. After, I had become a young woman, I can recall the change of Mrs. Annie, I never seen her drunk anymore and her words and actions had changed. She had been saved and was very busy in her community church. Yes, God changes things, when you let him in.

Again, only from a child eyes of my mother friends, Mrs. Lilia Blackwell, Mrs. Stella Nicely, Jean Bennett, (Mrs. Grace another best friend) Mae Hyatt and Mrs. Betty Colbert. They too share a special bond with my mother, wither it was in the church, community clubs or just shared whatever they liked about one another. I am unable to talk about them all in such depth, but I had to mention the names of her friends.

Third, but not less, maybe even the best of all her friends would be Sister Sadie Mae Kincaid. Mrs. Kincaid was a preacher wife, mother, choir member, bible study teacher, church and community board member and one of the spiritual earthly bodies that my mother needed. Yes, they were friend like all the others, but sometimes in one's life you need more. My mama needed somebody that, she could trust with, her spiritual guidance, her fears, doubts, weakness and just some encouragement to stay on the path of faith and the prayer from a prayer warrior such as Mrs. Kincaid. This I know because she did the same for me as a young woman in the church.

In my mid to late twenty, a group of young women in my community, we belonged to a bible study class that Mrs. Kincaid taught. I can recall Mrs. Kincaid talking about the teaching of the Apostle Paul and the loved she had for him; however, at that time, I was just beginning to study the bible. I could not share her understanding of the Apostle Paul. Now, I know what she knew. After his conversion into Christianity and Christ revealed to him his plans for us all, Paul wrote thirteen books in the New Testament on how we should live our lives and he wrote the most bible chapter, then any other writer. The Apostle Paul hated Jesus, and sought out to kill and did kill many, of Jesus followers. You see God will forgive anybody and can use anybody for his purpose and glory; not that God needs to, he chooses to. When

I think of Paul, I cannot help but to see myself. No, I am not a well-educated Roman Solider like Paul; nor have I written thirteen bible chapters or been in prison for Christ sake. However, I have lived a life that was not always pleasing to the Lord. And like Paul "I did not want to hear nothing about no righteousness," how could I when, my stinky thinking would tell me I am right. Mrs. Kincaid too, has gone on to glory and I am so glad that she was a part of our lives and I am probably traveling on some of her prayers.

My mother worked all the time until she retired and she had many different jobs. I can recall her being without a job, for only a short period of times; for whatever the reasons may have been. As I have already mentioned my mother was a strong independent woman, she was for the right; dealing with much but taking nothing.

My mother never said why she quit working for the Kilgore's I can only speculate. I can recall Mrs. Louise bringing her home earlier than normal one day, she did not often come home early. Then I notice for days, that she would be at home, when she would be normally at the Kilgore's. Then, I asked why are you at home? She just simply said, "I quit". I did not dare to ask why. I thought this was going to be one of these times, that she would not answers me and I might even, get chewed out for asking being a "busybody". Now, a few years later I am a teenager, I cannot remember the circumstances, but it had to have been about me. Something to do with some issues I was having. Anyways we were having this conversation. Then, she said to me "it does not matter how long or how deep your friendship is with white people, they will always somehow remind you that you are still black." With that beginning said, I thought, wow! Is that why she quit working for the Kilgore's. I believe Mr. Kilgore accused her falsely, maybe she overheard him saying something racist, or he made have called her the "N" word. I do not know but whatever it was, it was powerful enough that she would quit her job, that she had, since she was sixteen. knowing she had bills to pay and five children to support. In, yet she walked away. Whatever it was she forgave but never worked at their house again. Over the years, Mrs. Louise would come by and mama would go outside to sit in the car with Mrs. Louise for hours talking. Mr. Elmer, he too would come by on occasions to bring all the ingredients needed for her to make him, his fried apple pies. I also know the Kilgore's continue coming by during the holiday brings gifts and giving mama an envelope, which I am sure had money inside.

After working for the Kilgore's, I am not sure of what her first job was, I know she did work at a daycare center for a while, which was close to my elementary school, I can recall walking there sometimes after school and she and I would walk about a city block to Parker Drug Store to get a Hamburger and onion rings. She also worked in a factory called Peachtree Product. At the factory, I know she worked at night just cannot recall if it was second or third shift but I believe she worked the third shift. I cannot remember all the jobs she made have had, simply because I was getting older paying less attention to things other than my stuff. Now, if my memory serves me right her last two jobs was first with a lady named Marsha Love. I know my mother really loved this lady and I think it was more than her just being a nice lady, but a heart to heart connection of their similarity. Miss Love was a young single mother of two little girls, a working woman and dealing with women issues as well as life in general. My mother had already gone through where this lady had to go and I know my mother's heart she would sympathize with; all the things would come Miss Love way. I am not sure how long she worked for Miss Love; I know she worked for her until she moved away from Murphy, North Carolina.

The last job my mother had was with Bill and Sandra Forsythe; she worked for the Forsythe for many years and continues to work for Sandra and her new husband David for several years until she retired and from my understanding, I believe Miss Love and Sandra was kin some kind of way. Again, I say "God" always take care of his own and place the right people in your life at the right time. Sandra was a blessing for my mother and guess what, I know Sandra would say "no" B Dye was a blessing to her and I would say "we both right". At the time Bill a banker/ businessman and Sandra a teacher and owned an women clothing store for a while. The time mama started to work for the Forsythe's, I do not think they had any children, then they adopted Susan first then Troy as infants a few years apart and mama loved and raised them kids. I must share a funny stories mama shared with me when Susan was about two or three, not recalling the circumstance surrounding why Susan became so angry with mama accept a child's emotion, mama did not fold her blanket right, not enough jelly on a sandwich or giving her the wrong sippy cup. However, she said Susan got so angry that she started slapping her little hands together, beating the table and trying to speak, she was so angry she could not speak for a split second. Then, Susan said "B Dye you damn damn dumpy". Mama said that was so funny to her and unexpected she laughed so hard that she cried. Mama waited for Susan to speak, she had anticipated her saying the "N" word and had said to herself if this little girl said such, I was going to spank her good and I bet she will never use that word around me ever again. I do not believe Susan ever said the "N" word because my mama would have said so. Mama worked sometimes on the weekend for business or for children get away. Sometimes she traveled with them rather they drove or flew. Sandra and mama were friends, they shared many of conversation and I know when Sandra first marriage failed mama was a big support to her. I even worked for Sandra a few times babysitting and house cleaning. Again, I must point out another time, when God had the right person in our lives at the right time, with Sandra.

I had gotten into some trouble that I will get into later on in the book and moved to Atlanta to stay with my sister Irma Jean. I will never forget the generosity, Sandra showed us by giving me some new expensive clothes from her clothing shop, a coat, some pants, shirts and some other things. After mama retired, I think she may have done some work on a very rare occasion for Sandra. Also, over the years I have seen Sandra, we talk about many different things and of course shared many memories of mama.

In the early eighty, I attended Tri-County Community College. I had taken a Sociology class. In this class the instructor, John Cabe said that, we as human being behave a certain way for two reasons only, one being genes (hereditary) and the other is the environment in which we live. Now, I could believe those two reasons but for me, I had to disagree with that primes. Although my mother had three different set of children, the oldest girls had the same parents, lived in the same environment, so did the boys and Evon and I. However, every last one of us as far as personality goes, we were as different as night and day. I explained to him for that reason, I did not believe that. My argument was there having to be a third reason, called "self." From the moment of conception, "we are already who we are; when we came into existence." However, information we gather along life's highways, then we take on our own individuality; as for as personality goes. Although; we are constantly being "redirected," to take on others "selves," until we ourselves do not know who we are ourselves; molded. Yes; the other two reasons are most definitely so; the ways we are raised "reprogramed." The day of the chapter test, I missed that question on purpose because I did not believe the answer of just two. Some years later, I just happened to come in contact; with my sociology, teacher and he informed me; that my thinking was correct. That there had been some new studies about my thoughts.

Now, let me tell you why, I shared that particular story with you. I saw firsthand our difference as induvial, and I saw my mother's mothering skills handling each one of us differently even if the circumstances were the same. In the different had nothing to do with favoritism, but more to do with whom she would be dealing with. For example, Evon and Irma Jean were really tenderhearted, just a good scolding would work with them, they would cry and yes Evon was spanked too. I never seen Irma Jean spanked because of our age different, but I can say if you were a child of "B Dye" you been spanked. Even, as grown women, I have seen my mother grab, shove and smack my older sisters Fannie Mae and Lula Mae and a moment of their stupidity, the same with the boys, Willie more so then Ervin and Jerry and I got the most spanking of them all. Mama was so dedicated to us all; she wanted the best for us as well as being the best person we could be. She was the mama and gave us respect and she demanded respect in return, she use to say "if you can't control your own house you don't need one." Sadly, I say that is why so many Children are dying in the streets today because there are no more repercussions for bad behavior. Let me say this, the ways the law is set up today my mother would have been locked up, we got whipped with flyswatters, belts, switches, shoes, extension cords and whatever else I did not mention. Yes, those discipline tools sound horrifying and at the moment it probably was and yes, there are children being mistreated and abused every day all over this world, however there is a different in being chastised from real love, then from being abused from some demonic spirt of some sick individual. We were never abused. And the more you read my story you will see, if you do not, it does not really matter.

Her dedication to us was remarkable, on what she was trying to teach us about right from wrong and that there are consequences and repercussion on doing wrong and we did understand right from wrong, however many times we chose to do wrong, especially me. Now, days my personal opinion is; that this generation; really do not know right from wrong. The reason being, they have been allowed; to think right is wrong and wrong is right; they have no real rationalization. Okay; moving on mama had the most "sayings." Let me share some of them. For example, if I went against her warning of any giving situation and it did not turn out right, she would say "well you made your bed now laid in it," or "if that make you happy it tickles me pink." Then, there were the" sayings "when I was trying to be slick, telling her only bits in pieces of the truth, she would just look at me without saying a word, then I would ask, "do you hear me" her response would be; "yes, I hear what you are saying and I hear what you are not saying." I would just stand there looking stupid. Then, there were the times, I told on myself; trying not to tell on myself and she would say "a hit dog will holler." Then, there were the times; I would be having some kind of issues within the school or with the neighborhood children and she would say, "Sometimes you must grin and bear it" or "more you stir into shit the more it stink," or "chasing a rumor is like a dog chasing it's on tail it never catches it." Then there was the, "if you can live in it, I can live around it," or "I can show you better than I can tell you," or "that's your little red wagon you can push it or pull it," or "believe nothing that you hear and only half of what you see," or "one monkey do not stop a show," or "the word "if is like saying; if a bullfrog had wings it would not bump its ass every time it moved. I am sure there were many more, these are just the ones' that's stand out the most and as even an adult she would say some of her "saying" with different scenarios, and even now, I see them clearly as much wisdom and absolute truth.

She was supportive to us, for whatever we want it to do and

allowed us the time to do it, such as sports, girls and boys scout, volunteering for the red cross or community projects just to mention a few. The holidays were always special at the Brown's. On Valentine's Day we always got candy and cards to passed out at school and to friends, Easter a new outfit, basket and an egg hunt. On the Fourth of July Evon and I always got some new shorts, shirt, scandal, firecrackers and we all went to the county's fireworks show. Halloween maybe a mask, we normally just got creative making our own costume and she always pass out candy to the neighborhood children.

My memories of Thanksgiving and Christmas are the best; I can recall her starting in October buying extra food items putting the food in a box on the kitchen pantry shelf to prepare for the dinners. Both holidays, we always had the same side dishes greens, potato salad, pinto beans, green beans, and macaroni with cheese, corn, dressing, home-made rolls gravy and cranberry sauce. Thanksgiving, we always had turkey or baked hens, with pumpkin and sweet potato pies. Christmas was truly the best, we always had ham and fried chicken, but it was the cakes Mrs. Mattie Bell Jackson sent to us, Jerry and mama liked the pound cake, Evon and I liked the coconut cake and Willie and Ervin favored was the chocolate cake. Beyond the food it was the tradition, the boys would go into the woods to fine a tree until, they reach the age where they no longer cared as much, so I went to get the tree and yes, many was like "Charlie Brown's," however placed in the right position with the less branches against the wall and the decorations the trees where always beautiful. We would be awakening in the early morning hour on Christmas morning. We would be so excited as mama directed us to our on little spot of gifts, we always receive one gift that was not expected and overwhelming, such as a bike, movie projector, guitar, easy bake oven or child sewing machine, then we would began to open our gifts and every Christmas mama made each one of us a Christmas basket. Inside the basket would be several oranges, apples, tangerine, mixed nuts, peppermint sticks and chocolate covered cherries. My

Lord how much I miss those days, but I am so grateful and thankful that we had them.

There were three things my mother could not stand, one being one of us to be sick; and yes, she did her on doctrine, with her on remedies and they worked many times, however if it seemed not to be working, we went to see the doctor. Second to be mistreated, by one another; or an outsider; third we were not allowed to mistreat anybody. And yes, we did each other as well as doing others, as others did us and yes there were repercussion, "B Dye" did not play that. As you read my story, I will continuously share stories of such; however, at this very moment two come to my memory.

In the early seventy the county-built community center in each community. Texana community had been in service maybe a few years. I must have been about twelve, one day a few of my friends thought the center should be open, and we wanted to play inside the center. So, we posse up and went to Miss Mae Hyatt's house wanting her to come open the center, she refused, we cursed her out! Miss Mae called my mama and told her what I had done. When I came home mama asked me about it and of course I denied having anything to do with that. She did not believe me and instructed me to call Miss Mae to apologize for my bad behavior. When I hung up the phone mama was on me like "stink on shit" another B. Dye saying. It seemed to me simultaneously, "I hung up and she popped me so hard with a belt, I saw a flash of light." I attempted to run down the hallway but her reaction was like a western cowboy movie, throwing a lasso on a runaway horse. Now, I have had many spanking over the years, but that one will be in the top three and when I look back on that day, I wonder why I would have done such a thing; knowing Miss Mae would call mama. I blame it on mental illness.

Another story was when a neighborhood man would say hurtful things to me, such as "Mary Brown you should be called Mary Black, because you are so black you look blue" or "you fasted ass heifer." So, one day I cussed him out, I was tired of his remarks, he was so angry he chased me but could not catch me, then I thought it is time to bring B. Dye in on this situation. So, I told mama all about it, within a few days, he was walking down the road passing our apartment, mama called out his name and asked him to stop, she wanted to speak to him, he complied. She went into her bedroom and retrieved her pink pearl handle twenty-two maybe twenty-five pistol, and then she put it in her pocket. I follow her outside and stood beside her, she asked him about what I had said, he was like "oh no! Miss B. Dye, I did not mean any harm, I was just teasing her." She let him know, he was a grown man and that I was only a child and that this is the last time, they should every have this conversation again, he agreed, apologizes and kept walking. I am so thankful that my mother was the woman she was, she was all about peace and solving things quick and easy, however if he had got disrespectful or threatens, she would have shot him I have no doubt. As I keep sharing my life stories, I will boldly call out names, but at times

I will just tell the story, because they know who they are or because of family or friendships sake, no need in causing some unnecessary hurts.

Some years ago, I was watching a late-night comedy show on the television, when a comedian was making a joke about not letting the street light come on before he would get home. That was so funny to me, being that was a true rule for me. For my mama if that street light was on it was dark and I should have been home before dark in believe me, I was ninety-nine percent of the time on time. She was most definitely a "golden rules" mom. We always had to come home first from school or from whatever program we may have been a part of, take off our school clothes, do our homework and clean up the house. Her bedroom was off limits when she was not at home, however we did take the chance on occasion to go in her room for something, such as a needle with thread, scissor, scarf, her lotion or something along that line, however I was always amazed, when she would ask; "who been in my room." Standing there "likes a deer in a spot light," not wanting to admit but wondering, how did she know since I took every precaution to replace in time, in its proper place. Most of the times were forgiven, however you would be just reminded to stay out of her private domain. After we became older, she did not really care, then I asked her one day, "how you know when someone had been in your room, her response was "it is my room and I know if a dust ball is out of place." "Okay."

Her most steadfast rule was, if she had company you needed to go to your room or outside. I can remember a few times when I just wanted to be defiant and just sit there, so she would remind me softly to go play. Later she would remind me that, she should not have; had to tell me twice, and do not; do it again, then I did it again, this time after her company left she spanked me, the next time she spanked me in front of her company, the next time, she and I caught eye to eye, her eyes said to me "are you crazy, have you forgot or do I need to show you again." I got up and ran out the door. Needless to say, she did not have that problem with me again. That example along; reinforce to me all the many of reasons why "God" chose Beatrice Brown-Dye to be my mother, because he knew, whom he needed to trained me too. (Psalm 139:13-16) Since God created me, he knew me; he knew the wrong choices, I would live, however he protected me thru it all, now it is because of his grace and mercy, that I have this opportunity to glorify his holy name.

Thus far I have shared much about my mothers' love of church, her children, family and friends. I also talked about the era of her life, the men in her life, jobs and her strengths with wisdom. Like any other woman B. Dye had many favorite products that she would not wavier from, for me just remembering from my memory pool, I can still see these products, on her dresser, on the middle shelf in the kitchen pantry, or pulling her favorite treats out of her purse. Her, personal hygiene items were Secret deodorant, Dove soap bar, Oil of Olay, and Noxzema. Her favorite gum was Free dent's peppermint favor or Dentyne and candy Reese's peanut butter cup. She, bought for us napoleon ice cream, you know the vanilla; chocolate and strawberry mix, for her lime sherbet.

Mama was big on most vegetable, I can recall how she loved baked sweet potatoes which was like a snack for her many time midevening she would just bake one for her, then load the potato up with butter, I would just stare at her enjoying the potato and wondering why, since I did not like sweet potatoes then or now, we did have in common, not likening banana. Boiled okra she loved and would try to be slick by dropping a few okras into the pot of green beans, which we loved the beans but hated boiled okra; fried okra we did like.

There were many of times when it looked if as nothing was in the refrigerator to eat but when B. dye came home, those five weathered potatoes, one last soften onion, now is fried together, no bread but now, there is a hot pan of buttermilk biscuits and that slap of lean fatback meat is sliced, the salt boiled off then fried and re-warmed leftover beans dinner is served; or having a small pack of ground beef, not enough for us all to have hamburgers, but enough to brown and drain then combined with a can of green beans, corn, diced tomatoes and a cup of rice, we now have soup with a pan of cornbread. We were not scrapped most of the time but when we were, B. Dye made dinner happened.

Money being tight, she mainly bought off brand products, but she had to have her Tide detergent, "nothing cleans like Tide" and "nothing kills germs and make your house smell clean like Pine sol," she would say. "Okay," sure just mentioning two name brand products may sound a little silly and yes, she did buy others, however these two stands out in my childhood memory, just because I cannot recall when we were out of them, but believe me, we were out of a lot of things at times. (Proverbs 31: 17-21)

My mother's hobbies included jigsaw puzzles, knitting, making quilts, sewing, cooking, fishing and ball games. She made her hobbies ours, if you were interested and of course Evon and I more so than the boys. Mama would sit at the kitchen table putting a puzzle together, then transfer the puzzle to an piece cardboard box; glue it down, spread a light varnish over it, place it in a frame to hang on the wall, and yes I am right there with my busy little hands to help. Around the fall of the year, she would start making new quilts, from old clothes and any raggedy piece of cloth material she made have had, using a brown paper bag to make her different patterns, from circles, triangles and squares. Many of times, she would have enough of one or two of the same colors to make a quilt, however there were times she would use an assortment of colors placing them in a sequence that was so beautiful.

My mother no different than any other human being, she too had her on beliefs and opinions, on a variety of things, not to say right or wrong just her. I do not know of all of her beliefs or thoughts about everything however there were a few that we did talk about. When the subject of women having abortions entered into a conversation that we were having, I had the biggest shock, when she revealed to me that she thought it was alright to do. I immediately questioned her belief; after all she had had eight babies herself. Her response was, "if you are not going to love them and take care of them, an abortion in utero would be better than throwing the baby in a trash can; leaving along in an abandon building or something worse if possible." I understood for her that an abortion would be the best choice of the two evils. However, for me I would never say that an abortion is every alright. Yes, with modern medical technologies to say something is majorly wrong with the baby, some risk to the mother or rape and incest just to mention a few maybes. My personal opinion is, "if you lay down and get you should lay down to have," because most of us know how a baby is made and most know what's available to prevent unwanted pregnancies, that's the only right we should have as a woman. My reasoning is, "we do not know what; that aborted baby may have been. The one to have cured some of these diseases we have or could have solved some of these economic problems or whatever problems we are facing today."

One of many of her fears was mixed relationships for us; she understood that the heart is going to feel, what the heart feels. Yet, like the saying go "a fish can fall in love with a bird but where will they build their nest?" For her it was the danger of racism, especially for the era for her boy's safety and my brothers dated plenty of white girls. She was afraid for my brothers to be out in public with their "white" girlfriend, she thought that they may be attacked by white men hater and she knew some of the girl's parents did not know about their daughter's "black boyfriends" adding to the possibility of my brothers being killed by the girl's father; if he learned of the relationship. Even though she warned them, she allowed them to date the girls and they were welcome at ours home and of course, I have a story to tell about, one occasion further down in my book. My brother Willie second wife was white-Italian. Some of our children married or had children outside of our race and I am so thankful that all has been well thus far. "Amen."

We did have a conversation on "homosexuality," for her, she simply did not understand why the same sex would be attracted to one another and her curiosity was more from a sexual point of view, "what did they do"/how do they do what they do?" At the time of this discussion, I had no clue either, I was about fifteen and at that time most homosexuals were in the "closet," you really did not see much of it; however, you may have thought about who may be. B. Dye did have the "gay radar," she would predict in our own family, even the very young relatives; three or four years old, that they were going to be gay and they are. She did not judge, she was not a judgmental person and for her the reasoning behind homosexuality comes from somewhere within, from a place she could not comprehend and I can imagine her saying, "we do not have to know everything." Now, that homosexuality is so wide open and in many states allowing same sex marriages; she would be definitely shocked.

In October 1993, I moved back to Carrollton Georgia, with my two children and new boyfriend, Jimmy. We had met in the summer of 1992, when he came to Murphy, with a company to build a new water tower. I was really shocked, to learn that this stranger is from Carrollton also and that he knew my family members from both sides of my family. I had been separated from my ex-husband since October, 1991. I had just received my share in a lawsuit, we had found a nice house to live in, and both of us had new jobs, meeting new people, with an extra delight meeting people that knew my parents, having nothing but nice things to say about my mama and how "gangsterous" my real daddy was; but they liked him. Carrollton is a small town, but it is bigger than Murphy and only two hours and a half to drive away, therefore we did visit a lot and I was experience anew happiness. That lasted for eight years; the relationship, not the happiness.

After about two years, in Carrollton, when I heard this song playing called, "Dear Mama," by the slain rap artist, Tupac Shakur. I loved the song; I could relate to most of his words, the words sounded as if they were wrote for my very own mother, except for the part about his mama being on drug, my mama was never on drug, also the part about being raised on welfare, we were not raised on welfare, however we did receive some government assisting and last when he talked about him being in the penitentiary, none of us was ever in the penitentiary, however as you continue to ready my story, you made wonder how did I evaded it, I can tell you now, truly God's grace and mercy. In April, 1994; I called my friend Deacon/Choir Director, Roscoe Hall about wanting to be in the Mother's Day Program. I explained to him that I wanted to make a tribute to all the mothers in the church and some special words for my own mother, he supported my ideas, that I had shared with him and placed my name on the program.

On Mother's Day weekend May, 1995; I drove to Murphy with the kids for the weekend to participate in the program. That Sunday morning the weather was nice, the flowers inside the church was so beautiful, Deacon Hall and the choir were singing with such sincerity, everyone was dressed nice and you could feel the Spirt in the atmosphere, then the program was started. There were scriptures being read, a few poems recited, a solo being sung, pinning of the flowers on the church mothers and now it was my time in the program. I started by giving God thanks for all the mothers presented and pasted from this community and thanking Deacon Hall for giving me the opportunity to speak. As I began to speak, I called out some of the mothers by name, sharing quickly with them, how each had touched my heart. As I continue, I reminded the congregation although I am talking about my mother, I know I am talking about many of yours' mothers too. God fearing women, hard workers, strong, disciplinarians, concerns and with so much love for family, friends and community, I can feel your overflow and happy Mother's Day.

I began by telling the congregation about her "sayings," and my thought being what is this woman saying to me now. "This is your little red wagon you can push it or pull it." "You made this bed now laid in it." "A hard head will make a soft behind." Simply saying the choices, you make will have an effect and if the effect is not pleasurable, you just have to deal with it. I thought why did she just say that, and then I realized, she wanted me to think about what she had said, "figure out meanings of her words." I spoke of how, her calm manor could put you in check, you knew you had just been checked, however not a raised voice or a cursed word came out of her mouth. I must admit, I had rather got it that way at least, I would have understood; why I was feeling like hiding my shamed face. Then I began to read the words I had taking out of contexts of Tupac Shakur song.

"Dear Mama" you are appreciated
ain't a woman alive that could take my mama's place?
I was a fool with the fool breaking all the rules
I reminisce on the stress I caused
You always were a black queen mama
You always were committed a poor single mother (working)
tell me how you did it
There's no way I can pay you back
But the plan is to show you that I understand you are appreciated
Lady don't you know we love you? Sweet lady Dear mama
Place no one above you Sweet lady
You are appreciated
Don't you know we love you because when I was low?
You were there for me and never left me alone
Because you cared for me and I could see you coming home after
work late
You're in the kitchen trying to fix us a hot plate
You just working with the scraps you were given and mama
You made miracles every Thanksgiving
Now! I can reminisce because through the drama
I can always depend on you mama
With me when it seems that I'm hopeless
You would say the words that can get me back in focus
When I was sick as a little kid
To keep me happy there's no limit to the things you did and
All my childhood memories are full of all the sweet things you did for me
And even though I act crazy I got to thank the Lord that you made me
There are no words that can express how I feel
You never kept a secret always stayed real and I appreciate how you
raised me
And all the extra love that you gave me
Sweet lady and Dear mama Dear Mama you are appreciated.

As I read, I could see the smile on her face as she wiped the tears of peace and joy from her eyes. The glow on her face implying to me, "ok all the talks, spankings, punishments and prayers for you have finally worked." After the church service had ended, we mangled awhile talking about it all with those that had something to share with me. Later on, in the evening, we drove back to Carrollton taking my mother with us, she stayed for two weeks. While there, I took her to see people she had not seen in twenty or thirty years, their reunions were as beautiful as I listened to them reminiscing about shared moments. We went out to dinner several times, fishing, yard sales, flea markets and family gathering.

One day we were driving down Bremen highway going into the city, when she said to me "may-re, I don' believe I am going to be around much longer." "What?" I replied asking her what are you talking about you are fine. Then, I continue saying the cancer you had in your breast has been removed and that has been over a year now, with no problems. Then, she said "yes I know, but most of my friends are gone, my kids are all grown doing well with your own families." "Okay mama, I do not like this nonsense conversation." Then she said just let me finish. She went on to say, my TV and microwave give it to Ervin and Mattie Ann because they gave those things to me. I do not know what Jerry make want but whatever it is give it to him. Lula Mae do not want anything from the dead, but if she does give it to her. Give Willie my pearl handle pistol. I cut her off then, asking her are you crazy, that nut give Willie your pistol? We both laughed, then she said yes, he has always wanted it, give it to him and give him my CB radio so he can have a head start. We are rolling in laughter by now. Then, she told me she had a couple of insurance policy both are in your name and Evon name, not a lot but will buried me and whatever is left of money and things belongs to you and Evon. Then, I said okay mama, I will do what you have asked, but everything is fine. We went on with our day, I thought nothing else about it.

After, mama had returned back to Murphy a few weeks later, my daughter Mallari was ten; she had been in Murphy visiting her dad, when he brought Mallari back to me, she said "mama grandmamma is sick." I asked her sick how? She said her stomach was hurting? I did not think that much about a stomachache, because mama always kept over-the-counter medicines, for such as that and for colds, bug bites and whatever else. I thought she was probably lying down, I did not want to bother her and would call her later, and I did not. The next evening, my cousin Patricia Ann came to my house to tell me, that my mother had passed away. I lost it. After I got some of my composer back, I said to her, I did not know she was that sick and I did not call her, I felt so ashamed and sad. I wanted to go to Murphy that night to be with my sibling, but Patricia Ann said no, we will go in the morning; I did not sleep at all.

When, we arrived in Murphy and I learned that mama had been sick for days and was in the hospital, I became angry. I asked Evon why did you not called me. Evon said, "Mama told us not to call you, she said; "that nut will wreck and kill your fool-self trying to get here." I laughed and cried at the same time, knowing even in her death, she knew me well enough to protect me one more time. I knew in my heart she was right, I would have ran thru traffic lights, "the red ones" not stopping but yielding at stop sign, "okay" maybe not yielding either and speed limits sign, I would not have obeyed them either, that's if I would have seen them, I would have been in a daze and killed myself and maybe other.

I did not speak at my mother's funeral; I just did my best to keep composed. Her going home celebration was truly displayed as the queen, her flowers were beautiful and plentiful, Deacon Hall sung for me the gospel song, "Going Over Yonder," so many people, black, white, rich, poor, young and the old. The funeral procession was a twenty-two-mile drive to Hayesville, North Carolina to be buried at my pop's hometown; we were escorted in the front and in the back by Cherokee County Deputies. I do not know who arranged that and as we continue up the road cars were pulling over to side of the road paying respect, my heart was thanking every one of them and in my mind said "yes," B Dye you are so worthy, of such a pause.

I stayed in Murphy for about a week finalizing my mama's affairs. After returning to Carrollton the reality of my mother's passing creeped in and I thought how can I do this? Although, we did not talk every day, we did talk two or three times in a week and my thought was how am I going to make it without her? I was so sad, and then depression took over me, I was continuously crying, could not eat or sleep.

Then on my lowest day, I had to talk to someone; I called Mrs. Grace. I told her how; I was not doing well with my mother's passing and not sleeping, not eating and just crying. She said to me, I understand your pain; I went thru the same when I lost my mother. However, she said "Mary you know Bea would not want you behaving in such a matter as this; that will make you sick." Yes, she said moan but not too long, you have must take care of you for your kid's sake. We continue to talk for a while and yes, this was the conversation; that I needed and I started to call Mrs. Grace more often to see how she was doing and to assure her I was okay. Even though, I really was not and I cried literally for two years. My boyfriend, Jimmy saw me crying for the first time and asked me why are you crying? Between the tears, and sniffles, I managed to tell him why, and then he got used to seeing me crying and did not ask why?

And it took another three years before, I could just talk about her without crying and I still cry on occasions. Mama has been gone now for twenty-five years; I miss my mother.

Now, I do not know when, I came to the realization that even in her death was "perfectly orchestrated by God." The song that I just happened to hear; those words spoke for me. Then I had the opportunity to tell my mother, on "Mother's Day," what she meant to me and have done for me. The given chance, to spend two lovely weeks together. Surely, all of this had to have been a divine intervention, God's grace and mercy shinned on us, I cannot be nothing but thankful; for the thirty-five years we had and the peace in her soul, she wanted to go.

And I can imagine; when she stepped into, her father's house; he met her at the door and said; "well done welcome home my faithful child. She was so blessed and a blessing to those who knew her. At the time of her passing, she had birth eight children, had twenty-four grandchildren, eight great grandchildren, I have since stopped counting, their maybe seven generation of us now.

"My Sibling And I"

FANNIE MAE DYE-MOORELAND

WHEN MY OLDEST sister, Fannie Mae Dye-Moreland was born, my mother was only seventeen years old in 1938; turning eighteen that September. I am sure that her mothering skills were not what they were by the time I arrived twenty-three years later. When I was born Fannie Mae was married to Howard Moreland with three children, Tony, (Big Tony) Robert Lee, (Feet) and Alice Jean (Booboo) and had Mary Earnest (tiny) one month after I was born.

I did not meet Fannie Mae until I was eight years old. I knew about her because of my mother and other two oldest sisters Lula Mae and Irma Jean use to talk about her and I can remember asking them; where is she? They did not know exactly where because they had not seen or heard from her in years; but they thought she may be still in Atlanta, that's the last place they knew of her whereabouts. I can remember noticing that my mother would become sad when they talked about her.

Then one day a letter came from Fannie Mae to my mother, with her address and yes, she was in Atlanta. I can remember that day like it was yesterday, my mother cried and put the letter in a book, that she had made into a photo album. That letter was in that book for years to come, I remember reading it from time to time, now I recall it as being eerie. It was written like a poem or song, talking about wanting to "slip away." At the time of the letter arriving, my sisters Lula Mae and Irma Jean; boyfriends were two brothers Thomas and Simon Lloyd from Hayesville. This one particular evening mama was gone somewhere and they all had been drinking and decided to go to Atlanta to fine Fannie Mae. In the car were Thomas, Simon, Irma Jean, Lula Mae; her two boys Lamar and Wootche (Victor) and me. When they found where she lived, I was afraid. I had never seen such a dumpy house made into an apartment building before, we just walked into this building, and there was no door. In the hallway, I saw drunken straggled men lying on the floor; trash and rats seemed to be everywhere. We had to step over and around all of that mess to get to the stairway, when we reached her door and knocked; she asked who it is, when Lula Mae told her it was her; she opened the door and they felled into each other arms, then Irma Jean did the same. I just stood there. After all the formal who is who was done, I remember them telling Fannie Mae that they have come to get her. Then Fannie Mae told Tiny to get all of her things, they started grabbing things in such a hurry; throwing the things into bags. Then Fannie Mae said "hurry up she will be back in a minute." By then I had had enough of it all, from the building, the trash, the rats and the rush; something is not right. I ran back outside got into the car, rolled up the windows and locked the doors. When they came to the car; Simon unlocked the trunk so they could put their things inside. Lula Mae told me to open the door and let them in, I refused to do so; Lula Mae got so angry at me and said "if you don't open this door when I get my hands on your "black ass," I opened the door. After everyone was in the car, packed up like a can of sardine, we started to pull off when Fannie Mae looked back and said "there she is," I looked back too but I saw a man coming down the sidewalk.

After we had made it back safely to Murphy, my mother had so many mixed emotions. Joy to see Fannie Mae, happy that we were home and most angry, that they had been drinking and had Lula's two and me with them. I was in awe with Fannie Mae early on, was it the tone of her voice; maybe it was the clothes she wore; could it had been she was dark skinned like me or just me knowing this is my "sister." As I was adjusting; to them, Tiny was adjusting to us. Within a week Tiny had this mad crush on Ervin, mama and Fannie Mae had to explain to her, he is your uncle; you cannot like him that way; she soon understood and got over it. Now, Tiny had already heard, seen and done things, I knew nothing about. Within two weeks of them being there Tiny and I had a fight. We had been fussing about every little thing, the toys, the cup, the chair and who would get in the tub first and she was jealous of me invading her space with her "mama." At the time of our fight, we both were already fight ready, she had been fighting in the hood, and I had had several fights under my belt too. I tell you, by far the hardest fight; I had ever had at the time and I am assuming the same for her. We were literally fighting like two men in the streets. We fought so hard because of our own pride, I was not going to let her win and she was not going to let me win. I cannot recall exactly how, the fight got started, we were in the kitchen and so was mama and Fannie Mae and they just watched for what seemed like forever, then they finally pulled us apart. Then I remember Fannie Mae asking us are we done yet, or did we want to fight some more. We did not want to fight any more and we never had another fight.

My niece and I became closer than two peas in a pot; we came to understand who we were to each other and accepted it's okay to share our mother's love. I will share some more of Tiny and I later on; let's get back to Fannie Mae. Fannie Mae was tall and slim, nicely build; however, she did have battle scars on her body. She was always clean, mostly wearing skirts, with nice blouses and ballerina's shoes. She was sweet, friendly and had a happy smile, but she did not play and seemed to me she was never afraid, she tried to avoid nonsense but she had no problem in checking nonsense. After being with us for a while it's seemed that she had never been gone; she was at home.

A funny story; Fannie Mae had had an abscess tooth; the left side of her face was swollen. Wootche was probably four; he understood her jaw was hurting and he decided to pick at her, just being bad and threaten to hit her in the jaw. He was standing in front of her as she was sitting down; he would take a swing at her; she would lean back or throw up her hand to block him; she got tired of doing so; so she told him, I am not going to move again and if you hit me, I am going to beat the hell out of you. Wootche swung with his right hook; she did not move and his punch landed on her face. The punch was hard enough to rupture the abscess and the pain was so severe; she jumped up and ran to the bathroom, with tears in her eyes and leaning over the sinks as the pus ran out. Not long she came from the bathroom with a smile on her face; apparently that punch was what she needed at the time to release the boiled-up infection. She did not whip him; she thanked him but warned him not to every tried it again.

Fannie was without shame; she did what she did and said what-ever she wanted to say. Men seemed to gravitate to her and she loved being around men; she drunk with them; they enjoyed her company and spending their money with her and on her. As I look back now; I know it was her personality and what she was use to; expected and also; she was a new woman on the hill (Texana). She did also have a few women friends that she hung out with and they too were drinkers. I think many of the women in Texana may have considered her as less than them or just not on the same page as she; which was okay with her. Fannie Mae was so aboveboard; in all she was and if you were not ready for the truth do not ask her the question. I grew up to be just like her in so many ways.

I must have been about nine when I asked Fannie Mae, "How do you get a baby inside of you." I was traumatized with the answers. She went on to explained to me, how your body has to be mature before you can get pregnant. She went into great details about starting your monthly period; what it was and the age when most girls starts and "that's your body in the natural; but to get a baby you have to lay with a damn nappy headed boy and you stay away from them damn boys." Then, I asked "How does the baby come out." I think I had my mind set, that she would say the doctor would cut open your stomach to take out the baby. Then she told me how babies are born. The next day I told my closest friends; all she had said and I decide that day I would never have a baby and strangely enough; both of my babies were born by cesareans births.

A funny truth; Tiny started her mensural cycle three or four months before I did and I was jealous.

Three months was all I could take, I wanted to start mine too. I decide to get one of Tiny's pads and put ketchup on it and hide it in my room. When mama came home, I ran to get my pad trick and went into the bathroom; then I call mama into the bathroom too show her. She looked at me and said, "Girl you had better stop wasting my ketchup." Now that was crazy, I started my cycle the next month after three months of this new experience, I was tired of it; than being informed that this will last for the next thirty or forty years, I was really devastated.

I have already mentioned how my mother use to clean chitterlings in the backyard; squeezing the mess out of the pig's intestines, running the water hose through them and turning the intestines inside out. One evening while my mother was doing so; Fannie Mae was watching standing within the open door half of her still in the house but her head was out as she watched; she was eating a sandwich. I said to her; "Fannie that's nasty, how can you eat that sandwich and watch this?" She responded by saying, "Easily!" I am not eating that I am eating this." I just looked at her, then I thought, yes from that day forward, I decided whatever is going on around me if it is not me; it should not hinder me from what I am doing; another way of saying to me never be a wimp about nothing.

My friend Renee had gotten a new bike; one day we were up by the old Texana's school house; which is where the community center is now. Renee and I were sharing her bike switching time; she rides then I ride. I am riding to fast when I came around the curve; hitting a rock and lost control of the bike. I wrecked; I was hurt, I could not get up, I was screaming and crying. Renee ran to her mama's house where Fannie Mae was to tell her what had happened. Renee mama and Fannie Mae were friends and drinking partners and they had been drinking all that day; truth be told Fannie was drunk. Yet, she came to my rescue; she kept encouraging me to get up; I could not. She got me up on my feet, then kneeled down in front of me and told me to get on her back; she carried me approximately a city block; down the hill, drunk on her back to the house. She placed me on the sofa and elevated my right leg and stay with me until mama came home. My knee was swollen and hurting, and then this is what Dr. Mom did; she made me a heating pad by cooking some grits, she said the grits would hold the heat longer; then she pours some vinegar in it saying it would draw out some of the pain and swelling; stuffing the mixture into a sock then wrapping it in a towel. It did easy the pain as long as it stayed hot; she reheated the mixture several times throughout the night. The next morning; she knew I needed to go see the Doctor. What happened is that I had hit the ground with a direct impact to my knee causing blood vessels to snap and the pain and swelling was coming from blood that was pooling. The Doctor stuck a big needle in my knee and drew out the blood and squirted it into the sink; he repeated this probably about five or six times and yes, I was clowning; but I did recognize every squirt into the sink released more pressure therefore I endured.

No different than my behavior mama was not always pleased with some of Fannie Mae's choice but she was grown; she could do as she pleased in the streets; but when she was in "B. Dye's house or presents she too had to humble herself as a little child and Fannie Mae did not mind; they too had their own special bond; she too really loved our mother and had so much admiration for her.

Fannie and Tiny only lived with us a few months; when she and Tiny moved into our old house in the Hollard with Lula Mae and her boys. She was soon working at a restaurant/truck stop. Not sure of the time frame; however, Fannie had her first real relationship with Mike; they worked together and they started living together. I am guessing about a year maybe two. As I look back on their relationship from a child eyes; I believe they were fairly happy with each other for a while. Sometimes I would get off the school bus with Tiny and vice versa her with me. I enjoyed being with them all.

Then one day while I was there; Fannie and Mike got into a big argument and I have no idea why. She told Tiny and I to get our shoes and coats on we were leaving; after we got ready and were leaving walking thru the trail; he kept calling her name telling her to come back; she refused by saying nothing but kept walking; then he threw a rock hitting her in the back; she felled to the ground. Tiny and I was scared for her being hurt and was crying; when he came to close to her; Tiny and I bulk him. (not afraid tag team} He was cussing us swinging at us and we were doing the same. Then he assured us he was not trying to hurt her he was just going to take her back inside to lay her on the bed; we let him do so and followed him inside. After I went home, I told my mother what had happened; the only thing she said was "okay where is Tiny." Again, that was part of my mother's styles, her saying "if you can live in it; I can live around it." For about two weeks, I still went to see about her every day and she was still in the bed for three or four days until she got her strength back; then one day while he was at work she packed up all of her and Tiny things and moved back in with us. However, she was still working with him and me being me; being a little busy body; I would be listening and I heard her telling mama; he was bothering her and wanting her to come back; but she was done.

Early one Saturday morning; mama, Fannie and I was in the kitchen; mama was cleaning up the breakfast dishes; Fannie was sitting at the kitchen table drinking a cup of coffee as they talked. In our front room was a window that customarily had a chair or the sofa positioned there. I would constantly many times in a day jump on the chair/sofa to look out that window. Just to see who is going up the road, coming down the road; who is visiting and who is leaving. When I saw Mike pullup; I ran into the kitchen to announce that Mike is here. Fannie reached and picked up a butcher knife from the table; placing the knife beside her in the chair. I stood there with my eyes bulked, then turned to look at mama to see if she had seen what I saw; apparently not she kept doing what she was doing; then I looked back at Fannie Mae and she placed her pointing finger over her mouth to telling me not to say anything. I obeyed. Mike knocked on the door; mama invited him. He walked thru the front room and stood at the entrance into the kitchen; looking at Fannie Mae talking crazy to her; she never said a word nor moved. Mama spoke up and told Mike "that this is my house; do not come up in here with all that mess and disrespect. He was so crazed; he disregarded her words, unable to hear or care. He was still in a rage walking toward Fannie Mae; she jumped to her feet with the knife up in her hand and started stabbing him. My mama managed to get between them somehow trying to keep Fannie Mae at bay; he was not talking crazy at that moment just trying to get away from Fannie. He left; mama toe was broke; Fannie sits back down to finish her coffee and I am in awe of what just happened here. I can say that was the end of them; it was over.

By now Lula Mae is no longer with Thomas either; she has a new man Robert (Rob) and they stayed together for over twenty years. Rob was always full of jokes, trash talking and bragging on how mean he was; but in reality, could not whip a fly. He came to the house; this particular night being Rob playing with Lula Mae telling her how he would pick her up in power drives her. At this time the sofa was placed in front of the double side window; pulled out from the wall to keep the sofa away from the wall heater that was adjacent to the floor. We knew Rob was playing; however, Fannie Mae did not and took him at his words. Fannie grabbed Rob, I am serious; she picked him up, power drives him over the back of the sofa, he is trapped between the sofa, the wall and Fannie Mae; she is beating the mess out of him.

Mama and Lula Mae is pulling her off of him, mama is saying "girl what is wrong with you?" After she was pulled away from him, I do not remember any more detail about that night and I think the reason being, was because I was unafraid and I thought it was funny. After that episode all was well; Fannie Mae and Rob ended up being fairly close to each other.

Fannie Mae only stayed in Murphy about three years, and then she moved back to Atlanta. As I am sharing some of her life; I am reminded of my "Preface" the same questions for Fannie Mae's life. Why would God allow her much joy and so much pain? Then that question seems to be answered partially by this question; why did God give us "free will" to make our own choice? All I am saying is true the choice we make causes us much; then on the other hand the choice others make that is in our life causes us much. Not long after she had moved back to Atlanta; her new boyfriend shot her in her back as she was leaving my sister Irma Jean house; then Irma Jean boyfriend shot and killed him. Fannie Mae survived the gun shot. She was set in her own ways and she was determining to be in controlled of herself; that is why, I feel "not saying that they had the right," just saying the guys that hurt her from the back; was probably in her actions to imply "watch me leave."

Remember when we first went to get Fannie Mae and the rush to leave before "she" got back and then looking back thru the car back window, Fannie said, "there she is," but I saw he. Well she is he; her name was Mary Jo. I did hear her name being mention; however, I never thought anything about her nor did I ever ask any questions about her. Then one day Fannie Mae and Mary Jo just showed up for a day visit; I was happy to see Fannie Mae; and yet I still did not comprehend who or what Mary Jo was or what she was to Fannie Mae. After they had left, I did ask my mother about this "she he woman," I cannot remember what she said; that is even if she had said anything. Again, she did not understand herself so how could she explain it to me. It seems to me within a couple of months they came back again; Mary Jo told my mother that Fannie Mae had been sick and that she had not been eating, complaining with stomach pains and she had refused to go see a doctor.

We were thankful that Mary Jo had brought her home. Mary Jo left and said she would return in a couple of weeks to pick her back up. I think that is when I realized; Mary Jo kindness and her genuine concern for Fannie Mae; I really did not care about, their what, or their why; I only needed to know this woman cared enough about my sister to bring her home. She did start to eat some and mama was giving her some kind of over-the-counter medicine, that was in a small box that was black with yellow wording with some red at least that's how I remember it, in again Fannie refused to go see a doctor.

After a few days she went up to Lula's and Rob's house; what really happened after that only God knows.

Lula and Rob had left early that morning to go to work and Lula had said Fannie was not feeling well that morning. Lula had come home early that day but was unable to get in because Lula had locked the door on their way out the door; not needing her house keys because Fannie was there and could have opened the door. Lula said she had knocked and called out Fannie Mae name several times without a response. So, she went to her neighbor's house and had their son Kevin to climb into a window to let her inside the house. Upon entering into the house, she found Fannie Mae in Lula's bedroom on the floor. Fannie had soiled on herself and was foaming at the mouth, then Lula called the ambulance.

Inside the bathroom placed on the bathtub was a glass with a little bit of liquid left behind, with a spoon inside and the spoon was blackened; also, the medicine that mama had been giving her; which she had sent with her up to Lula's, was inside the medicine cabinet; beside some kind of poison.

I will always believe that Fannie Mae had mistakenly grabbed the wrong thing; and had poisoned herself, however, Lula has said she believes Fannie Mae killed herself and I have always believed, what a ridiculous thought; Fannie Mae loved life and she enjoyed living her life her way. Upon arriving at the hospital, it was confirmed that she had been poisoned, her liver was gone and her kidneys were locking. I can remember my mama saying, the doctor had said she had done all she could do; but just may be if Fannie Mae can make it to Grady's Memorial Hospital in Atlanta and placed on a kidney machine; she may live. That did not happen; on route to Atlanta just crossing the Georgia line she died. That same day Tiny was on the Continental Trailways Bus coming to Murphy; Fannie in the ambulance on her way to Atlanta; they passed each other going in separated ways. Riding inside the ambulance with Fannie Mae was Lula Mae and a male friend of Irma Jean; Morris Pendland and they were in agreement saying when Lula Mae said to Fannie Mae; "we just passed the bus; that Tiny is on;" she smiled, lifted her arm and then she died.

The day my sister died was April 16, 1975. I was fourteen years old, only knowing her for six lovely years. That day I had come home from softball practice, my pop was sitting on the porch and my niece Michelle was standing in the yard. I called her to me and said to my pops, "watch this lift and spin trick; that I have been doing with Michelle." I picked her up and did what I had being doing with her; when I placed her down and looked at my pops; I expected him to say something; such as that was great or stop doing that you are going to drop that girl and hurt her. Instead he had a complete blanked look and just stared at me with a sadness in his eyes, then I notice all the cars park at our house. I knew something was wrong. I then asked my pops, "where is my mama?" He replied by saying "she is inside," I ran inside the house there was my mother sitting on the sofa in the middle of two of her friends; she is crying and when I looked around, I noticed all of her friends and other people were there. I asked "what is wrong," then my mother said "Fannie Mae is dead." I remember first asking "who killed her?" My mother answered by saying; "no one she just died." I started screaming and took off running into the kitchen, crying and punching the refrigerator with my hands and head and I could hardly breathe. Miss Emma Cline came into the kitchen; she grabbed me and held me tightly as my limp body collapse to the floor and said; "Mary you must try very hard to control your pain, your mother needs you to be strong; now for her sake." I said okay and went outside to sit on the back porch to try to calm down and understand; the what, the how, the why must this be so.

I did not attend the funeral my mother had encouraged me to go; to an already planned camping trip in the Great Smokey Mountains; with a group of teen girl. The ride seemed to take forever; I was glad when we reached our destination. Getting out of the cars, putting up the tents, placing certain items in the cold creek to serve as our refrigerator helped some for a little while. Then the pain would recur and I would begin to cry again; Mrs. Peters our counselors took me for a walk to comfort in counsel me and for that I will always be thankful to her. The first night I remember crying and hoping this was all a bad dream; she could not really be dead. Then I became angry with GOD asking him why; Lord would you take my sister from us at this point in our lives? I did not get an answer at that time. Yes, I thought my love for camping could easy my pain and mine; it did not I yearned for my family the whole camping trip. Just another one of the worst times of my life.

I cannot really say for sure how long I did grieve for her and I feel perhaps not very long since I was a teenager doing teenagers things and I still had her thru Tiny. I never forgot about her and evening forty five years later; she still crisscrosses my mind. As children we never really imagine ourselves getting older; I never thought that I would really someday be a grown woman and if she had lived; I would had caught up with her just enough; that we would had hung out.

I am no longer angry with God that my sister passed away; I had to accept that is part of life; we all must die and he did answer my question of "why Lord?" The answer is getting out of your narrow box and look at the bigger picture; which is he did not have to let me know her at all. I could have only known of her, but God saw fit to allow me to know her for myself and cherish my memories; now that is good enough.

I do not know the circumstance of Fannie Mae and her husband divorce nor the splitting of their four children; what I do know is her ex-husband and his new wife raised, Fannie Mae's two boys; the second wife; already had three of her own and they had two boys together. The oldest boy Tony/Big Tony did eventual moved to Murphy, married and had two children; he also had another daughter in Atlanta.

They later moved back to Atlanta not knowing exactly how long; he had been in Atlanta when Big Tony got murdered in December of 1989. The murder was never solved. All we know is that he was shot three times in the shoulder, chest and in his neck. The other boy (man now) Robert Lee/Feet is still living in Atlanta. He is still living in their family house with one of his stepbrothers both parents have since passed away. Alice Jean/Booboo was raised by another lady; that I have never met; however, she did alright by Booboo. Booboo still lives in Atlanta; she has four daughters and grandchildren; she has been living in the same house for about twenty years and works at the Airport. Fannie always had Mary (Tiny) with her until she passed away.

Lula Mae Dye- Holland-Allen

As I CONTINUE to share my life with you the reader; understand even with the happiest of times comes with some hurts and pains and we have not gotten anywhere yet on my pains or my hurts. I must say writing about my relationship with my sister Lula Mae will be my hardest to write about thus far. Simply because truth is. Sometimes when we talk about things that are uncomfortable, we tend to "sugar coat" to soften the blow of the painful truth; I am not that person. If I can tell the painful truth on me then I can tell painful truth on others; that has caused me pain; at least what I chose to tell about others and how they have impacted my life.

Lula Mae the second born of my siblings, she was born, 1939. Again, she was twenty-one and already married to her first husband Milton Holland when I was born. Their first son Milton Lamar Holland (Milk Man) was born 1963; their second son Victor Lewis Holland (Wootche) was born 1966. Lula and the boys moved to Murphy around 1967 I believe. I loved those two-little boys; we grew up together and now that we are grown, we have maintained that same affection. I know the craziness in us comes from the Truitt side of the family tree; however; I had a double dose of craziness, from the Thomas's side of my family. As I was saying it is hard to control once going there; however, I have always been able to reel them back as well as them me. I really cannot remember every having to get physical with Lamar; but I do recall the one time with Wootche.

He was about eleven a big boy and I was sixteen. I was at their house; Lula was in the kitchen cooking; she and I was just talking and Wootche decided to be a little brat concerning me. He and I started fussing and I thought Lula would intervene on my side; she kept doing what she was doing. Then my pride(crazy) kicked in and my thoughts were they both must be crazy if they think I am going to allow my nephew to continually talk disrespectable to me. I grabbed him and I started tossing him around like a little ragdoll, threw him down in the floor, smacking his head. She stepped over us several times; continuingly getting her cooking supplies. He finally broke loose and ran out the door; needless to say, that was the first and the last. Over the years Lula and I did talk about that day; I was curious of why she did not intervene; her response was, "that was on you."

Lula and her second husband Rob had three daughters together; Kimberly Dianna Allen (Jippa Joe) 1970, Roberta Letitia Allen (Bert/Robbie) 1978 and Amanda Ann Allen 1979 When Kim was born; Lula and Rob was living crosstown up this steep hill that had a walking trail to reach the house; the house was an old wood house and cold like the brick house in the Holler. They too used an old wood heater; which kept the house warm as long as you did not like the fire go out all thru the night. If Rob or Lula did not get up in the middle of the night to put in more wood, it would be so cold the next morning.

I remember the very first day when they brought the new baby home it had been snowing and plenty of snow was all in the trail and I want it to carry the baby up to the house. Lula told me no; she explained the hill is steep and slick from the snow; you make fall and drop the baby. I started crying and saying I am a big girl, I want fall;

please I begged and then she handed me the baby and said "If you drop the baby????" I knew I better not and I did not and I loved that baby. Jippa too is grown now and has been thru so much; again, it is the choice we make and the hand that was dealt by others, however; she will always be my girl.

When the last two was born I was not around them as much when they were babies, I was grown. As they got older and I had babies; they were my babysitters but before they were babysitters my daughter Mallari was always at Lula's. Robbie was always a sweet mild child and even today she still has her same demeanor; however, she too can channel into the Truitt's. Amanda on the other hand was always a hateful child and she still is as an adult. The slack I give her is the same as I give everybody; I ask the question, what part of you has been impacted by your living environment or yourself? Sure, Amanda and I have had an auntie; niece relationship, however trying to maintain a relationship, with her has always been like pulling a tooth; I am not it. Around 2013 Amanda had come to Cincinnati to visit her mother; I knew she was coming I called my sister number to see if Amanda had made it there safely; she had then I asked Lula to speak to her. I heard Amanda ask, "who is it?" When Lula told her, it was me; I heard her say in a hateful tone, "what do she want?" My thought was wow what a statement; especially when I have never asked her for anything nor have, I ever done her any harm. My response to my sister was to tell Amanda not nothing then I hung up the phone that was it. Yes, I still love my niece; however, I bow down only to the Lord; that's her choice of behavior and her loss of pure affections; not only from me, she treats most people and family in the same fashion. All I can do is pray for her; life is too short to be so continuously unnecessarily bitter.

Even between the ages of seven and nine, I would still cry when my mama would leave with one of her friends and I could not go. I would just fall out. This was a normal Mary routine screaming, crying and running out into the yard so determined to go. I pulled this act quite often, there were times when mama would turn around or get out of her friend car and spank me; she may have chosen at times to take me with her or just leave me acting. Once I pulled that stunt while Lula was at our house, she came outside to get me, I ran inside the house into my bedroom got on top of the ironing board which was sitting upright in front of the window. I climbed up on the ironing board screaming and hollering out the window; I heard her ask my brothers for one of their belts, it is funny now; I heard about it later that they all three pulled off their belts. I was trying to get off the ironing board to run, I was late she whipped me off the ironing board.

Another time I cannot recall why I was going to get a spanking but like many times before I decided to run. I ran down the street from our house, the boys and Lula were chasing me; they could not catch me. When I got to the bottom of the street, I was in the fork of the road. I could have gone straight which would have led me into town or make the left which is Joe Brown Highway. I chose Joe Brown Highway. Lula threaten to hit me with a rock if I did not stop. I stop; not because of the threated but because I was afraid to be along on that winding road and at that moment the whipping, I had coming was the better choice. As I returned to Lula, she grabbed me and escorted me back to the house. My mama was standing in the door way; she is looking at me and I am looking at her; her eyes are saying, "I can hardly wait to get my hands on you" and I am thinking "please just do not kill me."

Lula too was a hard worker; working for years for the Dickey's that owned a hardware store and inside the back of the store they manufactory the Nehi brand soft drinks, that's the section she worked in also she worked in the owner's home as well as their son's homes. She also worked as a housekeeper in a local hotel and the town's hospital; she also prepared taxes for many in our community and she may have had other jobs that I cannot recall.

Lula's was the place to be on the weekend starting on Friday night for all the "happens," fish frying, playing cards, plenty of alcohol to drink and it did not matter what the era was rather in the eighty or ninety they mostly were still playing the fifty and sixty Motown records.

Even if for a weekend they went camping at the local camp ground, the crowd would show up at the camp site to keep the party going.

When I was about fifteen, I decided I want it to be grown and move from my mothers' in move in with Lula. I had been there for about two weeks; when I relized, I had made a big mistake. The grass was not greener on the other side. Lula had her own family; they had their own style and routine which was fine for them but not for me. I missed my room, mama, Evon; my personal television time and everything else I was used to. I wanted to go back home and my mother told me no; she reminded me, that I wanted to leave so stay gone. So, what I did was summoned Evon to help me in a scheme to ask mama if I could come spend the night with her; mama agreed and I took half of my things back home.

Within the next couple of weeks; I would spend the night bringing more of my things until I was back home and I never left home again at least not on a test run.

After I was grown in married, we still had the big sister-little sister relationship. A couple of stories to share of us being there for one another; one being Lula was always multitasking, making up a bed, putting a load of clothes in the washer and getting dinner ready all at the same time. One day she had called me to come take her to the hospital. She had let some cooking oil to get to the stage of about to catch on fire. She had grabbed a kitchen towel to enable her to hold the hot frying pan handle; as she was headed to the back door to throw the pan out; she bumped the washing machine and the hot grease splattered on her legs and foot causing second- and third-degree burnings. For several months, I drove her back and forward to the hospital every day for weeks, then as she healed; we would go only twice a week to once a week. This accident was very hard for us both and yet; we endured and she healed very well.

For me this is a funny story then and now. The late actress Farrah Fawcett was betraying a battered wife and a television movie called, "The Burning Bed." In the movie the actress ended up killing her abusive husband by setting the bed on fire while he was asleep. Since I too was in an abuse's marriage at that time; she called me the night of the movie to see what I was doing. When I informed her that I was watching television; she immediately asked me what was I looking at? I told her a movie called "The Burning Bed," she too was watching the movie and she want it to remind that, "this is only a movie do not get any crazy ideas." We laughed and I assure her it is okay; I am not having any crazy thoughts. After we had hung up the phone my mother called with the same question and advice.

Looking back, I cannot recall us planning any thing together. It was always family orient, community happening or something she or I may have been planning solo; I am sure the reasons being age different and our likes being so different; plus, the truth being our personalities often collide. Even, so I thought I could always count on her and her me and we still can; however, with her there is always a price; like rolling dice even if you seven, she has a way of turning your dice roll into snake eyes and I will just let that statement will reveal its self as I continue to write.

As I share more about my sister and I; I have to ask this question again; "what part of you is really genetic, environment or self?" Genetics you cannot change, environment and self you can; but only if you have a willing heart by listen to others and look at your own self with truth. She is immovable on her own life stances; she can see others shortcomings in her eyes only, but can never see her own demons. However, I must give her the same benefits, that I have given to myself; by asking the question, again "what has happened in her life that she has allow to mold her as her?" What I do know is that she moved away from our mothers' house at the age of sixteen and never returned and started drinking early on and still drink heavily; but she is not an "alcoholic" so she says and keep in mind; my truth will not be her truth. She is the kind of person that seems to love negativity. Anything that is negative is not negative enough for her.

In the early ninety a neighborhood woman burned several men

with gonorrhea; that truth is bad enough; not for her, she claimed she got a letter from the health department saying it was "Aids." Now that I am saved and drug free those two facts are wonderful to my family. She has tried to make even that negative, now to her I am "HOLY MOLELY" and with malice on occasion will remind me of my drug addiction, which is ridiculous; I do not need remaining, "I lived it; I claim it and I am writing about." For me to tell all the un-sisterly acts, she has done to me, would be a book within itself; of how she kept a little boy overnight for weeks while a woman I thought was my friend was sleeping with my husband within a month of our separation or riding with a another woman to my apartment whispering to my new man; that she is with a woman that wants to be with him for the night; or maybe for three years she tells me, when I am ready to move back to Cincinnati I can stay with her; until I can get reestablish.

Although, after giving up my place in North Carolina and had sold most of my things, she stops answering her phone; I went anyways staying for four days with a friend. Then when I went to her place, she treated me so unkind for two weeks; that her daughter and boyfriend could feel the negativity in the atmosphere and invited me to stay with them and I did for four months until I got my own place. I do not take her behavior personally; because I am not the only one, she has treated some of our other siblings and some of her own children with some of the same emptiness, just different scenarios.

Lula also has a way of always trying to separate us as brothers and sisters. Sure, there are three fathers of my mothers' eight children, which does not change anything as far as still being brothers and sisters. Granted, the bonds may have some differences just because of ours timing, ages or genders; that's it and that's all.. She has made so many statements such as, "my sister referring to Evon to me and vice averse saying your sister to Evon referring to me." She has also said to me many of times, that "her sisters are dead," which is true; however, they were sister to us all.

One day making that, "my sisters are dead," statement; I asked her "have you ever wondered, why they are gone and you are still her." Her response was "yes I have," however; she did not elaborate on what her thoughts were. Then I said to her; "it may be that God is showing you mercy, giving you more time to change some of your ways." She responded by saying, "good I hope he keep giving me more time." I did not say another word; I just looked at her and let my mind wonder. And it was not about what she said; it was more about the tone in her voice and the vibes I felt; it was as if she was saying, "I am not changing and if that is the case, I hope; he will keep letting me live." My siblings and I do have a stubbornness about us; however, Lula has this invisible brick wall around her; that no earthly one can get thru it to reach her and that is sad. With all that has been said; I love my sister and she me; although it is only with a level that she is capable of loving; she has said to me many of time, "I am not your enemy." Which says to me deep down she knows she has caused me some harm.

Lula stature is every bit of four feet tall and one-hundred pounds; however, her sizes did not affect her ability to defend herself. I remember as a little girl she too was always fighting, boyfriends, husbands and other women for whatever the reasons may have been; however, knowing Lula; not all but most was probably her doing. Lula truly has away had a way about herself that will make the humblest person have the desire to slap her; although I would not advice that. Lula is never wrong, yet she is wrong most of the time.

When I was about ten or eleven Lula and Fannie Mae had had a fight. They were in Hayesville, North Carolina, I do not know what the fight was all about, but I am sure Lula provoked it. When they arrived at ours house, Fannie Mae had a towel with blood on it placed on her head, Lula had hit her with a rock. My mother was upset that they had been fighting and I was mad that Lula hit Fannie Mae with a rock and I said so. I cannot recall why they had the fight; however, I do remember why Lula hit Fannie Mae with the rock. Lula told mama that Fannie Mae had her pinned to the ground and was trying to choke her to death. Lula said while on her back, she fumbles around on the ground until she felt the rock and hit Fannie with it to live. It was apparent to me three things, one Lula's voice was hoarse, Fannie was winning and sister or not defend yourself by any means necessary.

When I decided to write about my life, my family and friends has been very supported accept Lula Mae. I am sure her concerns are that I would make her as a villain. Again, I just have to say truth is and that there is good in the worse of us as well as bad in the best of us; she is who she is. She is still being blessed, November 2020 she will be eighty-one, she takes no prescription drugs, she can still walk without a Cain. Also, for me, I must say fair is fair, only talking about how she has caused me pain; therefore, I must talk about all the aggravation, that I placed on her during my drug addiction later in the book.

Irma Jean Dye-Lloyd

My sister Irma Jean was born October 1941, she was my mother's third child. Irma Jean was tall, skinny and her completion was what they call in the black community, "high yellow or red." She was also very reserved. I must say it does pain me very must to talk about her and the reason being, I do not believe my sister was ever happy and that is not to say she never had happy days or joyful moments. I think like me she had a lot of hurts and I do not believe she ever came to terms with her hurts; Irma Jean was a drinker; she too numbed her pain with alcohol and normally she drinks alone, playing her music, dancing and would talk during those moments.

I can remember hearing her saying that Lula and Fannie use to make fun of her because she did stutter in speech at times and they would tease her saying, "you to light, daddy is not your daddy." In again I say "what pain have we caused others?" And yet, what's even worse is when one does not have the ability or knowledge to know you can let go of the old hurts and not allowing those hurts to limit you. I am not saying the two examples alone was her only hurts. I have no way of knowing what else could have hurt her growing up and her choice of men was surly much of her hurt.

My best memory of her as a child was sitting on the front porch with her as she drank coffee and smoked cigarettes. This Red bird, would land; on the sidewalk and peck it's beak; on Irma's car rim. I asked her why is that silly bird always pecking on that hard tire rim. Her response was that the bird is seeing its reflection; on the tire rim and the bird thinks there is another bird there. This was our early morning routine; just to watch this bird beat himself up; then the bird would fly away and come back the next days, for a while. One morning the bird did not come, I was upset about it; in her laughter, she said his peak was probably sore. The next morning, I waited for my "little Red bird," to come the bird did not come it never came again. Wondering aloud what could have happened to the bird; she said to me maybe the bird founded a real bird friend. As simply as this memory is; it is one of my fondest memory that we shared and even today; I relive that memory when I see a Red bird. As a child I can recall Irma Jean lighting her cigarettes with soft book matches and I thought it was so grand; because she could swipe one match one time on the strike zone; then I would try to do that, however I would swipe the strike zone over and over until the soft cardboard and the match would be falling apart.

Irma Jean was a standoffish person; she did not like a lot of conversation or questions asked to her; nor hearing you asking questions. One day we were in the kitchen and mama was frying some chicken. I was standing nearby, enough to see that when she turned the chicken over there was some white slime bubbling. I asked my mama; "yuk what is that white stuff?" Irma Jean spoke out and said, "why you so close; what does it matter you will eat it when it is done." Mama jumped her bones with the quickness. Telling Irma Jean to shut her mouth; she is not talking to you; she is talking to me and how else can she learn anything without asking? Mama continue on scolding her on her attitude; she did not say a word; but I knew her feeling was hurt; she was so vulnerable.

As I continue to search my little girl memory box of her, I cannot recall of her having a "best friend" and again that is because, Irma Jean was not friendly; she did not trust people and she communicated with others as least as possible. Her life was always centered around mostly her family, children and her man at the moment.

Irma Jean in her husband, Simon lived in Haysville, North Carolina and they had three children together. First born Simon Vincent Lloyd Junior born, 1969 Michelle Lee born, 1970 and Gregory, born, 1971. Their marriage did not last very long; Irma Jean left her husband when she was pregnant with Gregory and moved to Atlanta. I can recall my mother being very concerned about Irma Jean moving to Atlanta with the children and yet she was grown and could make her on decisions.

Over the years, Irma Jean would come bring the children to visit us and sometimes leave them for a weekend or a few weeks in the summertime and mama would allow their dad to see them. Irma Jean had good children. They were well mannered and obedient toward their mother. Now they are grown, have their own families, hard workers and have mild demeanors; however, they can and will handle their own. The three have my highest respect and love and I have the same love in return from them. I do not see them often; we all live in different states; however, when they were teenagers; they would seek me for advice and still can and do. Reasons being, they knew I had probably "been there done that," and that I would not lead them wrong and that they could trust me with their secrets.

Her first relationship that I can remember was with this man named Junior. I could sense that mama did not trust this man and she was fearful of him being around the children; she said so. This man was from the city, he seemed hard and for my mother; Irma Jean was well out of her league with this one. I do not know how long they were together; nor all the circumstances that surrounded; Junior killing Fannie Mae's boyfriend. Shortly after the killing, she did move back to Murphy for a little while then returned back to Atlanta.

When we met her new man, Clarke; he seemed to have had a meeker personality and was a soft spoken man. He worked and would bring them up often to see us and I do not know the time frame of their courtship, when the children started telling my mama in telephone calls that they did not like him and that he was fighting her. Irma Jean "sugarcoated" the truth dismissing it as a misunderstanding from the children. My junior year in high school I had gotten into some trouble for fighting and pulling out a knife; which I will also talk about later on in my book. It was because of that incident, my mother sent me to Atlanta to live with Irma Jean; she wants me to finish school. Within a couple of months, I saw the abusive myself. I could not understand why she would stay with this man. The house was in her name, she received state money and food stamps; for her and the children. She prepared meals every day and kept her house spotless, never went anywhere and every morning when she would wake us up for school; we would have to make up ours bed as soon as we got out of it.

Clarke had a cardboard, paper and plastic junk business; whereas he brought those things to her garage and she would separate the items in their own categories for sale to be used as recyclables. I know he did not give her much of the profit even if any; that was one of many things that she argued with him about. Again, I am now out of my comfort zone and constantly intervening in their mess. I am also beginning to despise this man and I am afraid for him and myself because I know what I was capable of doing to him. However; I knew I had already failed again and I must control myself just to finish school.

Then one evening I was getting ready to go to a Saturday night school event and she had been drinking all that day. Now that I was dressed and ready to leave; she decided that I could not go and me being me; I was not going for that. We began to argue. I recall saying to her, "you have known about this night for a month and I am a young girl and if your choice is to stay home all the time and let life past you by; that's you and I am going." She grabbed me, throwing me against the wall and then she slapped me in my face. I stood there looking into her face; contemplation on what to do; but my pity for her redirect my thoughts so I walked away. However, she was not done; she grabbed me again from the behind pulling me backwards, then I turned around picked her up and gently laid her on the kitchen table and then, I ran out the back door, crying. I must say as I recall upon that day those same feeling has reappeared; therefore, at this very movement the tears are beginning to flow down my face. I was crying for my sister. As I ran my thoughts were, she is like a fly caught in a spider's web; she can see the spider coming but she cannot escape and as much as I was hurting for her situation; it was not mine and I was not going to be denied nor trapped and such a lonely place as she was. However; within a three years period; I would be the fly.

Within a few weeks of that incident I moved out. I had met this girl Jennifer Grant (tee-tee) within a three-month period of me being in Atlanta; we had become close friends. She and I met as we were walking to school. I needed someone to be my friend and again God had to have been looking out for me to meet my opposite and yet, our friendship grew and our trust in one another grew, then I begin to share my living situation with her and she had shared with her mother. Now I had been over the Grant's home many of times and then one day when Mrs. Grants asked me would I like to come stay with them? I was shocked and I just looked at tee-tee; I knew she had to have told her mother something. Then I told her yes; but we would have to ask my mother.

I called mama and told everything that was going on and that I too wanted to finish school and told her what Mrs. Grant had offered; then I passed the phone. Mrs. Grant and my mother met over the phone and they talked for a while about the situation and I know my mother schooled her on me, questioned her about my safety and her taking in another child; she had six with four still at home and grandchildren. When they were thru talking, they were both comfortable with their arrangements. I stayed with the Grant's and finished my junior year, then I returned to Murphy for the summer and went back to the Grant's for the start of my senior year. Again, look at my God's hand, placing the right people at the right time to see about me. I never stopped going to see my sister, playing with the children, walking to the neighborhood store with them and they kept coming to Murphy.

May, 1984 is another day I will never forget. I was driving into the city limits of Murphy and Lula and Rob were driving out of the city limits; when Rob began to honk their car horn and they were both flagging me to pull over. Although, that was usual behavior I had no thoughts about it; I had had a good day and things were great. So, I pulled over into old Brumby's Textile Mill Company parking lot and Lula got out of their car, walked over to my car; then she said, "Irma Jean is dead." I heard those words immediately. In an instant, I was gasping for air and it seemed to me that my car was closing in all around me. I opened my car door, I jumped out, I began to scream and I took off running up the street. Again, Lula has to chase me, calling my name telling me stop and asking me where are you going? That was a good question, it was at that moment that I just stop and fell to the ground crying uncontrollable. While I was on the ground Lula did encourage me to get up and pull myself together for mama and Irma jean's children sake; so, I did. We went back to our separate cars and went to mamas' and within a couple hours; I drove my mother to Atlanta. That same day of my sister's death; my brother Jerry; his wife Fannie (Maine) went into labor with their second child. That day Jerry was truly between a rock and a hard place; wanting to go with the rest of the family to Atlanta; but needing to stay with his wife for the birth of their baby. However; his wife insisted that he went with the family assuring him it was alright with her and that he needed to go with his family during this difficult t time and he did I am not complete sure but it does seem to me that, he did get back before the baby was born; this was truly a bitter and sweet day; we lost one and gained another, on the same day.

Irma Jean had laid down to take a nap and she died in her sleep at forty-three years old. At the time of her death I was a young grown woman, I understood clearly that we all must die when it is our time and I do think for the most of us; when we lose someone special to us; we need something or some idea to help us cope with our lost. How I cope with her death, my first thought was "at least she won't have to hurt no more, can't no one hurt her anymore and how sweet it is to go while you are sleeping." My second thought was, "I am so thankful that I did not hit my sister back that day; which has brought me so much peace over the years.

After the funeral; she was laid to rest in Atlanta. The children were fourteen, thirteen and eleven and Irma Jean had always said, "if something happen to me, I don't won't my kids in Hayesville with their daddy and his family." Most would think she was simply a woman scorned; however, I know it was more sinister than that. Their father came for them; he and mama talked about it and she had asked them what did they want to do? They were unsure and stayed in between for a few weeks; but their dad was promising them the moon and the stars and the two oldest went with him and the youngest stayed with mama. I was furious. I reminded mama that Irma Jean did not want her kids in Hayesville and I told their daddy the same thing. Needless to say, he and I did not communicate much after that for years; however, we got over it enough to be casual toward one another, he too has also passed.

Mama stance was; he is their father and if he wanted them and if the kids wanted to go with him; she was not going to get caught up in a war of words nor the courts.

Remembering my sister's deaths; by re-tapping into the pain of it, I now realizes, I never thought about the pain; that my mother had to have endured; to have lost two of her children and again, I can only say "showing her strength and faith;" not questioning the "why," just trusting in God to see her thru. Also, in thinking about my three older sisters, I have had to come to realize the era of which they came and at that, time my mother was only twenty years old with three little girls and she herself was really only a girl. I am sure she had to have been a different mother, being her age, leaving a dysfunctional mother,

MARY & A-HALF

entering into a dysfunctional marriage and not having an "how to do book." Now I have learned that there is really an "how to do book," call the Holy Bible. I still have no doubt; mothering those girls, were fair and her best because they too; adored our mother a well.

JERRY BROWN

MY BIG BROTHER Jerry, my mother's first son born, 1954 was truly the sweetest, kindness and most humble person, I have ever known. He called me "sis" and he would always say to me, "sis picks up your damn feet." I had and still do have the habit of dragging my feet at times when I walk, not as much so now.

I have never seen him fight; (except the guitar incident) nor have I known of him to be caught up in a lot of nonsense, but I have seen him; in all his meekness being willing to put it aside if necessary for me; but mostly controlling me to abide; to his wishes and I did only for him; just because of my love for him, as I remember. As children growing up Jerry was always the good-guy and he cherished his role as the "big brother,'" he was mostly an "A-B" student and was chosen as most athletic his senior year, 1973 because of his basketball skills and in his youth; he made his mama proud. When we were younger; I would tease him by saying, "be careful because you know you are allergic to cars." Jerry had been hit; by a car twice. The first time was when he was about nine.

The story goes, we were still living in Carrollton, Georgia in the housing projects. Jerry and some of his friends had made themselves some box cars and they were riding their cars in the road when a car hit him. Beside some scrapes and bruises he was alright and I remember my mother saying that the police officer had said his box car had been made really cleverly with strong Iron surrounding the boxes, which protected him. Is it really necessary for me to say, that was the end of the box car driving?

The next time Jerry was hit by a car, he was probably around the age of twelve or thirteen. That day Jerry and Willie had been up the road (Texana) hanging out, they were on their way home; around the corner just above where we lived. Willie come busting into the door telling mama Jerry had just been hit by a car. I remember mama was sitting on the sofa watching television while peeling some potatoes. I was sitting on the floor in front of her with my hands out catching the peeling. Just something for me to be doing because she had a bag there for the peelings and some water in a pot for the peeled potatoes. Just some me time. She stood up and asked Willie where is he; Willie replied around the corner, the three of us ran up the road and Jerry was lying in the ditch. This white man that had him was so apologetic. He was explaining how Jerry just step out in front of him and how he had tried to dodge him. He hit from the behind; Jerry was on the wrong side of the road; we had been trained to walk facing the traffic. I remember the man picking jerry up putting Jerry into his car and mama got in too and they took Jerry to the hospital within a few hours they returned home and again he was alright. What still stand out in my mind about that day; my mother saying she does not know what happen to her knife, she never found it. She searched the peelings bag, walked back to the spot and asked the man had he seen it in his car because for weeks to come the man would stop by to apology again and make sure Jerry was really alright. The reason the lost knife so embedded into my memory is because it was strange to her; that she was so frighten, she could not recall what had happened to the knife.

I can only recall twice; that Jerry and I had an argument. One being; Jerry was never the "Casanova" type of guy; but he did have a few girlfriends during his teenage years and I believe his first real love was this white girl; Kathy. I must have been about twelve or thirteen, when Kathy was his "girl." It was the fall of the year; dark came early and the temperature was cool outside. The front door was closed but not locked and the living room light was off. When I enter into the house, I was running in a hurry to reach the bathroom. The sofa was against the wall and to the right of the sofa was the hallway to the bathroom. Being that I was in a hurry, I was running and pulling off my jacket simultaneously then I pitched my jacket onto the sofa hitting Kathy. I heard her scream out, but I still had to use the bathroom, therefore I kept going. When I came out of the bathroom; that is when he angrily told me that my jacket zipper had hit Kathy in her face. I apologize. He did not believe that I was really sorry and accusing me of doing so, on purpose out of meanness; he said. "That made me so angry." I had apologized from my heart, now he is accusing me falsely and I felt betrayed, "he choosing this girl over me!" I went directly into my "crazy zone." I cussed them both out. I had many cursed words between my remarks; of saying "you two should not be in the dark anyways and why is she always over here; go over to her house sometimes; oh, I forgot your black ass not allowed at her parent's house." I said what I had to say, then I went into my room and they left. In of course he told ours mother own me and she scolded me for my behavior, however I did not get spanked; she believed it was an accident and she just accepted my frustration.

The second time was when mama had helped Jerry to get him a car. Jerry and a few of his friends were going out of town to some sport event and I convinced him to let me go with them, since it was his car; not his friend. After being on the road for a while, the boys fired up a joint. (weed) I must have been around the age of twelve or thirteen; I was so afraid. I got started, accusing them of trying to kill me; also stating we all are going to jail, hating the smell on my clothing and that the smoke was getting into my body too. However, I was not saying those things in that tone; I became so irate they had to put it out and I never asked to go with them again, until I was on their same page. (smoking weed)

I cannot recall Jerry being in trouble often with our mom; yet again I was probably just unaware and again we kept secrets from her. I think, Jerry must have been around sixteen when he started sneaking around smoking cigarettes. One-night mama was gone and Jerry was smoking in the house and again, I am always climbing on the sofa peeping out the window, when I see mama walking across the yard only steps from reaching the door. I warn him, "here comes mama." He panics and stuffed the cigarette down into the side of the sofa mashing it hard and quickly to hide and hoped the cigarette was out; he failed. Within minutes the sofa was smoking, (laughing) mama quick removed the sofa cushion and poured water on the burning area, which was not yet in flames. Upon seeing the cigarette; she asked who was smoking, with pause Jerry admitted it was him. I do not recall her saying another word, until the next morning; when she asked him what kind of cigarettes does, he smoke? He told her what he smoked. When she returned home from shopping that day, she had bought him two packs of his brand and said to him, "I bought these because now I know, you want stop and I do not want my house burned down."

Jerry did have many friends, although Oscar Allen was truly his best friend. The two were together often, but again I was in to me, therefore, I do not know much about their times together stories. Soon after graduating from high school he attended Tri-County Community College, however at that time the college was only a Trade School and he learned how to become a land surveyor and soon started working for Felix Palmer's Surveyors Company and which he worked for them for over twenty-five years.

I cannot recall the year, when Jerry married a girl from our community, Fannie Mae Smith-Brown, (Mamie) however I must have been about fourteen or fifteen years of age. For the first several months of their marriage they lived with us and his wife did not like me. At family times playing cards, watching television, eating super or just talking; she never had nothing to say to me and even would pull out of the conversation many of times; when I got in them. Then one day it happens, it was something that I said or done and she began to laugh uncontrollable; from that day forward; not only was she my sister in-law but a trusted and loyal friend; we loved one another.

After they moved out into their own apartment across town; I can remember all the summer nights and snowy winter nights that we would walk together from their place to ours. Years later I asked Mamie; "do you remember, when you did not like me and why." She said because of your "mouth." What? Was my response; my mouth? She went on to say; your boldness saying whatever you thought not caring about the effect of your words. I responded to her by saying; "well that has not changed." She said to me; "no you have not but that is why I love you." "You are who you are and you are just crazy enough and real enough to say what you please." That conversation between us happened over forty years ago; since that day, I have learned even to this day; that the people that love me or despise me is for the same reasons. You see people do not want to hear the truth; they had rather you kept silent, sugar coat the truth or agree with the lie they tell themselves and I am not her. I must say; those whom loves me is a hundred to one; that do not. As for my haters; I am sorry for you; you chose to missed out on all the love in joy; I share with everyone, from my real heart and guest what; I love you anyways; but I can "feed you with a long handle spoon."

Jerry and Maine stayed together for over twenty-five years having two children, Bridgett Dinah Brown and Bridgett was the first baby born in Cherokee County of that year. Then their son Jerry Chaz Brown was. The children are grown now with spouses and children of their own and are doing very well, I am so proud them. Bridgett was always my little girl; I was her babysitter a couple hours in a day and often on some weekend nights. I started calling her "Pep Pep Louise" I still do and I am the only one that call her that. After Jerry Chaz (JC) was born, I had my own baby Mallari a year later. They were two peas in a pot. When, they were around four and five; we bought houses side by side.

One day I was in the house probably cooking, when I heard Mallari scream, I ran to the door to see what was wrong. JC had Mallari by the hand running so fast toward the house that her feet were literally off the ground of every other step. I ran to them to see what was wrong; JC said "I was swinging a metal pipe around in my hand and the pipe hit her in the head." Directly in the center of her forehead was a small gash and it was bleeding. After I cleaned and stopped the bleeding, I did not think it was bad enough to take her to the hospital. JC was so afraid for Mallari but he was also afraid that I would be mad are Maine would whip him; he kept standing near the bathroom door saying, "I didn't mean to." Then I said to him; "I know you did not mean to and I am so proud of you; you did a brave thing; you did not runaway and you brought her to her mama." When Maine learned what had happened, she wanted to spank him anyways just for swinging the pipe, but I asked her not to and how brave he was, so she did not.

Jerry never changed as far as being meek and mild in manners; even when he was drinking. He would be annoying by repeating silly things but never mean. Mama knew he enjoyed a drink; she did not know how he behaved when he was drinking. I do not know where he could have been or how she would have been able to see him in his "drunken state ;" but she did and she said to me; "if anyone had told me; that Jerry could be so silly; when he was drinking I would not have believed them." In later years his friends that he drank with gave him a nickname, King-Can. The Miller's High Lite Company was producing a large thirty-two ounces can of Miller's beer, that was his drank. When he would be drinking his favorite saying was, "oh well" no matter what. If you said to him, "the ballgame has been cancelled because of the ran his response would be "oh well." If you said to him, "Nate was in jail, Paul had a car wreck or Sally and John got married; his response would still be- "oh well." In reality, I guess that was his way of saying "so be it, it is what it is" but it was how he said it was hilarious; how he would have bobbed his head and extended those two words. (oooooh welllllllll)

Jerry drinking finally took a toll on his twenty-five years of marriages; he was essentially a weekend drunk. He went to work Monday thru Friday and would start to drink Friday night until six o'clock Sunday evening to begin sobering up for work come Monday morning. Even though his wife moves out they stayed friends and co-parented their son.

I was living in Dayton, Ohio when I learned that Jerry had slipped in fallen up in the mountains while surveying in February, hurting his back and for days he stayed at Lula's house in pain. Lula eventually forced him to go to the hospital, he had not been to see a doctor in over twenty years. At the hospital they did many tests on him and found a knot on his back near his spine. Upon seeing the knot, the doctors decide to shrink the knot with radiation, which in turned paralyzed him from waist down and then they informed the family that he had cancer and put him into the nursing home.

I came home to see him; he seemed fine to me; he told me he will be alright and was dealing with it all very well. Our brother Ervin would go to the nursing home to sign him out taking Jerry to Texanna; for a little activity. I returned back to Dayton and then our town Murphy, North Carolina and our Community Texanna did what they do for their own. I believe it started with the secretary of Palmer's Surveying Company. They started with a grand fundraising campaign to help him with all of his expenses. For the next several months the family kept me informed on how he was doing and he was deterioration.

As painful as it is for me to admit at that time, I was so deep into my drug addiction, I really did not hear them and when they sent me money to come home I did not. One evening my niece Robbie called me and said to me, "if you want to see your brother before he dies you better hurry up and get home." I heard that. My "sugar daddy" upon me telling him my situation, he immediately took me to the grey-hound bus station, in Dayton, that night to catch the bus to Cleveland, Tennessee where I would be picked up by my family; to be driven to Murphy.

I arrived in Cleveland at 10:45am on a Wednesday morning; there to pick me up was Evon, Maine and Robbie. After hugs of greeting; we loaded up; headed to Murphy. As we were riding; one of them said to me, "you need to prepare yourself; before you see him; he has lost so much weight; he looks like a starving Ethiopian." I did not say a word. When we arrived in Murphy; we went directly to Murphy Medical Center. When I saw him; I was glad; that they had prepared me; because it was so. Standing beside his bed; grabbing his hand and I called out his name; he opened up his eyes and looked at me; then he bucked his eyes as a way of saying, "do I really see you?" I laugh at him and then I said, "Yes, it is me; I promised you I would come." I never left his side after that; except to use the restroom or peep out into the hallway. I slept in a chair beside his bed for two nights; he was able to speak, although his speech was very low basically a whisper. He was unable to eat or drink; so, I used the hospital's large saturated lemon-flavored Q-tips to keep his mouth from being so dry and continually putting lip balsam on his drying lips.

Again, I must share God's awesomeness Grace, his Mercy and his Faithfulness thru all of this. While I was in a layover at one of the bus stops; on my way down, there was a folded Christian Pamphlet laying in a chair beside the chair; that I was sitting in; I picked it up and put the pamphlet into my purse. I pulled the pamphlet out and being to read it to him; he just looked at me and his eyes said "thank you." Then I embraced his hand and begun to pray with him. You see for me even in my deepest uncleanness and living in the way; that was not pleasing to God; I knew enough about him that in spite of me; God still loved me and I could still pray unto him.

After the prayer; I told him; Jerry you are a good person; you always were. You are humble, generous and I have never known of any malice in your heart. And yes; you made have not been going to church; like we did as children; but guess what; God searches the heart and yours overflows with compassion and that is good with God. Then I said to him, "go it is okay; you don't have to worry are hurt no more." When you see the bright lights walk into it. Within minutes of our conversation a nurse came into the room and *gave* him a shot into his thigh, I felt bad for him for a split second then I remember he is paralyzed; he cannot feel the needle stick. I asked the nurse what was she giving him; she said, "the monitor informed them that his blood pressure went up; which meant to them he was in pain." I did not comment; but I smiled because I knew; his blood pressure went up because he was excited by the "Good New" I had shared with him.

Not long after that a friend of ours; Preston which is Jerry's best friend Oscar's brother and our brother Ervin's' brother-in-law. As Preston came in, we embraced; he went to the right side of Jerry's bed and I stood on the left side and we both held his hands and talked to him. Then, we began to talk with each other in our same positions, holding Jerry's hands and looking at each other, then we both looked down at him at the same time; Jerry had stopped breathing. I shook him and called out his name and ran out into the hall to summons the nurse and at that very moment; Jerry's daughter Bridgett came around the corner; I our eyes met; she knew and she screamed and collapsed to the floor. I ran to her and joined her on the floor; then I began to encourage her to stand up and she did; then we returned to his room and started to calling all the family.

The family choose to have his funeral, at the funeral home to be able to seat they expect family and friends; which was the best choice, many came. The saying "may the work I have done speaks for me," was a true statement for my brother; his person; the crowd represent that. As Reverend Oliver began to officiate Jerry's funeral; he said "I had visit Jerry several times during his last day and I could not understand why nor how but God; he was still hanging on. Accordingly, to Reverend Oliver he said, Jerry told him, "I am waiting on Mary to come to see me; she is coming." I immediately thought; what "conformation." It was not by chance; that I founded the pamphlet; it was not by chance that he bucked his eyes with joy; upon seeing my face; nor by chance that; we had the opportunity to see each other and pray together; for God had already orchestrated it all; with his amazing grace and faithfulness. I Praise his Holly Name.

The funeral was sad with many tears and the spoken words of memories of the speakers and then I thought; I have to compose myself and say something, then the words; just came to me. As I stood up and looked around at everyone there; I first thanked them for coming; then I told the mourners about their being eight of us and Jerry was the first boy. Then, I said. "I have learned in funerals, that people cry for two reasons and two reasons only. One being you did not love that person enough; to show nor tell them of your love and now the guilt and the shame are piercing your soul deep within; but too late." "Two being because you are "selfish" and that is the tears we are having right now." "We are not really crying for Jerry; we are crying for us; ourselves, "selfish." "Because we did love him right and he us; but we are crying because we no longer have him to talk with, laugh at, laugh with, get money from and hangout with anymore; so stop crying; stop being "selfish" let go and be thankful that he does not have to suffer no more and just know we did love him right."

Jerry left this life May, 2003 and his wife Fannie Mae Brown (Maine) passed away fourteen months later on July, 2004; she too had been sick with cancer too; but her death was still shocking; she was doing well and we had just lost Jerry. I can only imagine the grief Bridgett and JC had to bear to lose both of their parents within a year of each other and JC was in his early twenty going to college. I just know the Lord gives and the Lord takes away. In Ecclesiastes 3: 1-8, there is a time for everything. God is still good. Bridgett and JC have been truly blessed; they are both marry; their children are health and they are financially stable. Jerry and Maine would be so proud of them.

WILLIE RALPH BROWN

WILLIE OUR MOTHER'S fifth child and second son, was born 1956. He too was an outstanding athlete and was chosen most athletic his senior year, 1975. When he graduated from Murphy High School, the school retired his jersey number twenty- two and his rushing yards has not been broken thus far. There were so many colleges interested in him; offering him a free ride to come play for them. The colleges sent coaches, athletic directors and whomever else; to try in convincing him to come and play for them. They came so often bringing films of the school, some of their games and whatever else they had to persuade him. Of all the school; to come mama had want it him to go to Clemson in South Carolina. He chose not. I am not completely sure of what it was about Clemson that mama wanted him to go there; however, I am completely sure why she did not want him to go to the school that he did chose, Appalachian State and Boone North Carolina. Again, I say mama was the kind of mother, that would give you advice; from learned experiences; whether the experiences were her directly or indirectly, then she would allow you to make your own decision.

I do not know the reason or reasons he made have had; not to choose Clemson. However, I am very sure why our mother did not want him to go there; it was all about a girl. We that have experienced high school know; that it is common; for, the most popular boy to date the most popular girl. As mentioned before; Willie was the football star and Lucy was the captain of the cheerleaders. The issue for mama was, Lucy finished school first in 1974 and she too went to Appalachian. Mama's thinking was; that, they were both young and from a small town; therefore, the picking up, of their relationship is slim to none. She wanted him to understand; Lucy had a year head start on him. A year without him, away from Murphy, a larger town, new people and boys that would be equal to or and some ways maybe greater than him; at least in a young girl eye.

However, when you are young, dumb and in love you; just think and you do not hear none of that. However, the reality of mama's thoughts came true; they did not work out. And mama other reason was giving yourself a chance to be in a new place and maybe you will find someone that is equal to or maybe in some ways greater than she. Willie eventually left Appalachian and attended Berea College in Kentucky. I cannot say for sure if that lost relationship; was the cause of some of his out of control spiral trips; but I do believe it was one of them; however again it is still the choice he made. But then; again, Willie has always had this Holly-then-thy attitude.

Willie was always popular with the ladies so much so; he has had two wives and six children by three different women, at least that is what we know. His children are Tameka, Wesley and Michael; their mother is Anna; then there is Bradley his mother Betty and his first wife Patricia they have two Leona(floss} and Anthony.

Now, that I have finished making known of my brother Willie; let me share our relationship; we have never gotten alone; too long. As a little girl between the age of three and eight; as sharp and as clear as my memory is, I do not remember any togetherness with us. No memories good or bad. My memories of Willie as a little girl of about nine; until

I was around sixteen and our relationship was not pretty; he literally hated me, I thought; I hated him too; that's is he got back what he gave me. However, deep down in my soul, I only want, him to love me. Now that I am a grown woman looking back at my life, I can see why; we could never get along. The truth is Willie was really the "Bully" of us all; he thought that he was smarter, the greatest, and everything had to go his way; that is why he and I did not get along. I have always had the attitude "if you do not bother me, I want bother you" and I had the "mine set" of what was right, what was wrong and what was fair. However; Willie did not care about none of that; it was always about him and I was not having it, truly our personality clashes. When it came to the other three; Jerry, Ervin and Evon; they mostly went along with his nonsenses to keep the peace especially Evon; however, the boys would buck back on occasions; me; I always buck back.

Unlike most households today, we had only the one television and now that I am looking back at this story I am going to share; I must now laugh about a time when our televisions were already not in the best of shape. We once had a black and white showing picture television; that you could not turn the volume down; so, mama had a piece of cardboard taped over the speaker to lower the sound. I can also remember having two televisions to make one; one was used for the sound and the other one was used to watch the picture. However, in time my mother did buy us a nice colored television and we had to share the television. There were programs that we all liked and did watch together. However, as a "rule of thumbs," whomever cut the television on watched what they wanted to watch; until you went into your room or went up the road.

Willie had the habit of it did not matter what you were watching when he came home; he would just turn the television and if one would say, "I was watching that," Willie would say, "you were." Now, Evon and I loved, Elvis Presley movies, I must have been about eleven or twelve; she and I was watching an Elvis movie; he came in from up the street and turned the television. The same routine; we say to him; we are watching this movie; he response the same, "you were." I jumped up and turned the television back; then saying; "we still are." So, now; he and I are turning the television backwards and forwards; until I got tired; then I decided okay, "nobody is going to watch the television.'1 I went into the kitchen got the butcher knife came back into the living room, unplugged the television and cut the cord into; which was a bad decision. When mama came home, I explained and gave her the piece, I had; she used some electrical black tape and fixed the television and spanked me; in hood style, "beat the grab out of me." I do not recall what happened to him; but knowing my mama; he did not escape either. Willie and I was always fussing and fighting and the older we got the meaner the fights got. I cannot remember all that had happened; but he angered me so badly so often; I cannot remember what the fights were about. I remember one fight going into the boy's room to retrieve Willie's things to destroy. I broke some of his trophy, cologne and threw some of the same across the street into the woods; while he watched; it was over; I was crazed and he knew just to watch the; "Mary show." And of course, when "B Dye" got home; I am sent into the woods, to retrieve those things and yes; another "beat down." Willie and I would have physical fight all the time and the fights were vicious; I have chased him up the street many of times with whatever, I got my hands on.

Since we were all ways into it; I am not sure why; we started to argue this particular evening; I was standing in the kitchen doorway; getting a hot bowl of soup; the bowl was in my hand, when he threw a shoe at me; I moved quickly out of the shoe way; he threw it so hard that it but a dent and a crack into the hall closet door. I look back around the corner and when I saw the dent; I thought "he tried to hurt me," it was over; I walked over to him and pitched, that hot bowl of soup on him; all he could do was run past me down the hall to pull those hot soup soaked clothes off. At this point, there is no need and talking about the ramification when "B Dye" got home except it was not about me this time; but about him, busting the door and the fact if the shoe had hit me; I would have been seriously hurt. I can remember, she beat him with her knuckles.

Tiny and I must have been around nine or ten; mama was at home. Tiny and I had been up in the woods behind our house, clearing a spot with mama's rake; we had nails, the hammer, cardboards and a large rusted barrel; half of that day; We were making us a clubhouse. The barrel was beginning to overflow with branches and leaves, so we decide to burn them down; to make room for more; the plan worked. Now that the area is clear; we began to nail the cardboard to the four corners of the trees; the club house is finish; so, then we went back down to the house to get our old curtains, a metal folding table, a chair and other supplies, all gifts from mama. We returned to decorate our clubhouse and played in it for a while; upon returning back to the house a few of our friend dropped by the house; they were walk-ing to town; so, with permission from mama, we went with them. We had been in town for about an hour and we were headed back toward Texana; when we heard sirens going off; we all wonder; what could be going on in Texana. We started to run just to hurry to see, then we saw; the woods behind our house was on fire. Tiny and I thought the fire in the barrel was out; so, we had dumbed the burned leaves out. We were terrified. When I walked into the house; Willie said to me; "yes you did it and mama is going to beat your black ass." I began to cry; not because I was worried about the whipping; but because I did not mean to do it and he was getting so much joy out of my fear.

I ran thru the kitchen out the back door into the yard where my mother stood, watching the firemen put out the fire. I just dropped to my knees in front of her; telling her I was so sorry; it was an accident and that Willie was calling me names and he said; "you are going to beat my black ass." She just reached down grabbed my hand pulled me up and said; "no I am not; I know you did not mean too, then she walked into the house; put her finger in Willie's face and said to him; "I am sick of you always messing with that girl; you leave her along." Although, that made have worked out for a little while, but it did not stop. She did what she could do; he was whipped, talked too, talked act, punished and I am sure pray for too, but we fought for years. And then again; I have to said mama was a single mother doing the best she could with how she could; but she could not be there twenty-four seven. I learned early on; she did not have to be; I could defend for myself.

Of all the fights; Willie and I had, there was this one comical fight over a biscuit. Every day when mama would come home from work at the Kilgore's, she would bring home their left overs. While she was in the kitchen putting the food down on the table; I was going thru the wrapped food picking what I wanted. My adult sisters, Lula Mae and Irma Jean was in the living room with their boyfriends. I cannot recall who else came into the kitchen to get some of the food; it was never a lot of food and it was not going to be our super. I had made me a plate, fried potatoes with onions, a pork chop and "the biscuit." I never was much of a bread eater, but on occasion; I wanted a piece of bread. Mama had left the kitchen and was in her bedroom, probably hanging up her sweater and putting away her purse. Willie being Willie came from his room into the kitchen; to see what mama had brought home. While he was looking and getting what he wanted, I was at the refrigerator getting me some Kool-Aid; I turned around to see him getting my biscuit out of my plate. It is so funny now; but at the time it was not funny. I screamed out "put my biscuit back;" he did not; now I am all over him, he is holding the biscuit and with his arm extended up; I cannot reach, however I am jumping up and down trying to reach and screaming; over and over again saying, "give me my biscuit back." Mama heard the confusing and came out of her room and made him give it back. For years to come and even till this day; Lula Mae reminds me constantly on us embarrassing them in front of their boyfriends over a biscuit. Again, for me it was the principal of the situation; if only he had asked, I would have given it to him.

In even with all of the fights; we did take time out to trade favors; to defend and complement one another on rare occasions. In the early seventy, the Afro was the hair style to have and all my brothers had one, but Willie always wanted his perfect; therefore, he would have me to hot press his hair and put lose braids in his hair; just for him to take back down later to have the perfect round, full and soft Afro and for two dollars; I would iron something for him.

Although, I liked my Christmas gifts; I wanted to play with my younger sibling toys too. I was allowed to many times; but Willie never. However, if he was gone; I would play with his toys. My favorites toys of his was a movie projector; I would be in the boy's room, push their hanging clothing to the side of the walk-in closet to project the movies on the closet wall. Then, he had this electric football set; whereas you could line the players in position on the metal football field; placing a small rolled up piece of paper in the running back arms; which represented the football and if touched by the defensives player; I would have to realign; now it is second in twelve. I loved that football set and I played with it for hours. Willie also had this blue bike, if he was gone without the bike; I would try to teach myself how to ride a boy's bike and when I conquered the task; I knew I could use the bike for leverage someday. I cannot remember what he wanted me to do for him one day; but whatever it was, I told him; I would only do it, if I could ride his bike. He responded by saying, "girl you know you cannot ride that bike." That is when I told him; that I had been practicing on his bike, for a while, when he was not at home, so I showed him, I could ride and the deal was made.

Willie, did not have to defend for me often; I was more than capable of defending for myself.

However, there were times when I did have some troubles with some older or bigger boys ever now and then. I would tell him about it; however, I would throw in a little "white lie," saying the boy throw our mother's name into the mess; that would for sure send him to go check the situation. Again, needing him to defend me, was far in between; the neighborhood boys did not want to deal with Willie anyhow; he too was mean. I also can assume he checked situation that I did not tell him about; he must have heard thru the grapevine (town gossip) the bullying, toward me just stopped; I knew it was him. Now, we were capable of double team others if necessary, as well as double teaming one another. However, we had this unbreakable bond; whereas we may fight amongst each other, but no one else could fight one of us without hearing from another one of us.

One afternoon Willie was outside in the front yard bench pressing some weights; I am outside too. He must have been around sixteen and I would have been about twelve. He pressing a lot of weight, up and down; he stops and add more weight. I am watching and deep down I am so proud of his strengths, but remember; we do not like each other. Then the unexpected happens; he does not have the strength to lift the weights back to the rest bar. I am looking at the situation and he knows he is in trouble and for a split second; I just looked at him and he does not ask me to help him. I just ran to him and grab the weights and together we lifted the weights back to the rest bar and he did thank me. The position of the weights would have crushed his throat. That situation was one of the moments that I realized; I really did not hate him as much as I thought I did.

For me; the feeling of him really loving me was far in between. The first time that I can really recall was when a tornado hit Murphy sometime and the seventy. Of course, it is needless to say how terrifying that was for everybody. In again me being me always listen to what is been said. I overheard Willie talking to mama; he was trying to convince her too go to the fallout shelter and when I heard him say "take Mary and Evon with you; we will be alright; (the boys) my heart melted; he mentioned my name; he does love too.

Again, we loved sports and I loved to watch him play football. Willie was so gifted as a player; his strength and quickness as a running back was truly amazing. I have missed seeing the quarterback slip him the ball; then you knew he had the ball; the defenders are chasing him and he is weaving in and out like a maze; then when he would get to the side line it was over. I have seen him be five, ten and maybe more yards from the goal line; with several defenders wrapped around his waist and legs; he just dragged them in with him for the touchdown. I do not think I ever missed a home game, that he played and I had the blessed opportunity to go to most of the out of town games too; so thankful to my friend, Lori Shook and her parents, Ann and Harold.

I must stop at this moment to share about them which in term will shine a light on my town Murphy's people. The Shook's was a fairly wealth white family; they owned the cable company and Lori was their only child; she and I was as different as night and day in every way. Yet, we were friends; I was in their home many times and the out of town games; they would come pick me up, pay my way into the game, paid for my food, bring me back home and never ever made me feel less then. They loved me; for me and I loved them because they loved me. The Shock's have passed away too; however, I have seen Lori over the years since our childhood and I have had the blessed opportunity to tell her what they meant to me.

Now, I must say Willie was very protective of Evon and I as we got older and the boys was zeroing in. (wanting to play doctor and nurse) He would tell mama about me dancing with some boy to close, at community dances, house party or at the community juke joint. He would even confront me at these events; I am sure Evon too. However, I did understand where he was coming from; with his concerning's; from a boy's view point. (boys will be boys) At fifteen I was the shapeliest girl in our community, Murphy; even perhaps in the state. (laugh out loud) Marilyn Monroe the Iconic star figure was considered the best shaped woman of all times; her measurements were thirty-six, twenty- four, thirty-six. My measurement at fifteen was thirty-six, twenty- three, thirty-seven; my waistline was smaller and my backside was larger.

At that age my hormones and curiosities are racing, like any other teenager and I knew I "had" a beautiful body. One night as I was getting ready to go to this party; Willie got started. I remember saying to him; that he needed to shut-up; I reminded him of all the other girls that he had been with, slipping girls in and out of the boy's bedroom window and that they too had brothers; none were sacred in your eyes;

nor did you care what those brothers may have felt and I am not sacred either. At that moment of conversation; I actually got a clearing of sorts from him; he did not like it; but he shut-up; he had to realize; he has no control we were going to have boys liking us and we could like them back if we wanted too. Now, remind you Evon and I had already been taught at an early age about boys and living with three brothers; we understood boys and the do's and the do not's; plus, mama had embedded in us no babies.

Now, that I am looking back on all of us, the gap between Willie and I was always there and from the age of seventeen until I was twenty-four; I do not recall any communication with him at all and the reasons being are many. One being; we never communicate much anyways; therefore, our presents was not missed by either; I am assuming. Second being; Willie was not around me; I am in Murphy or Atlanta and he is in Kentucky, Ohio or Georgia either; he just living in one of those states or going to school.

When I was twenty-three; I had been married for four years and the marriages had not been very happy. However, at this point of the marriages things was well as far as I knew. My ex-husband and I were getting along, I am deep in the church and I am having a baby. Willie, my ex and even I was childhood friends to my ex; they had a special bond, playing together, spending the night, playing school sports, skirt chasers and "want-a-be-thugs." I had to share this bit of information, just to set up a clearer understanding of my relationship with God at that time and how Willie and I was so void but the closeness of Willie and my ex-husband was still strong.

Within a couple of months of me having my daughter;(Mallari) in 1985; Willie had returned to Murphy. Willie came over to ours house one afternoon and called my ex (Larry) outside; he just wanted to talk with him for old times' sake. After some time had passed; Larry came back into the house; wrapped up the baby and took her outside so Willie could see the baby; by now, I was really tripping within my thoughts. Willie left and Larry returned inside with the baby; then I asked him; "what was that all about?" Larry replied by saying; "Willie said to me; he wanted to see my baby." I was so hurt; not ours baby; not my sister baby; just my friend baby.

I just walked away into our bedroom without saying a word; I closed the door; sit on the bed and I cried like a baby. As the tears ran down my face; unpleasant childhood memories began to cause my heart to flutter and then a thought came to me, "get on your knees." I got on my knees and began to pray with a sincere heart intense prayer. I asked God to intervene for me; I need him to fix this long overdue of hatred, pleading for relieve and peace. God is so awesome; within days, Willie came back to the house and this time he knocked on the door and asked if he could come in; my response was of course you can; "come in!" He began; by saying to me; that he just wanted to talk to me. We talked for hours; doing our best too interpreted our behavior toward one another, then we embraced; we had a new friendship and for the first time ever; we acknowledged our love and that we are brother and sister.

After me asking God for his help; Willie and I developed a relationship that lasted for twenty-five years; without a hoarse word and that's not to say we did not have occasional disagreements; we knew we could share our thoughts, make jokes, give gifts of money and have secrets. One day while the three of us were hanging out at the house; when, Willie said to my ex; if I ever need a fight partner; "I had rather have Mary on my side then you." My ex responded by saying; "I had rather have her on my side then you." I laughed, but my thoughts were this is not funny. "Lord have mercy on me;" I knew and they knew how crazy I could become and as I continue to share my life; you the reader will to wonder; "why I am not dead or spending my life behind prison walls," and the answers is; "BUT GOD." "But God," is so true; Willie once said to me, that I was so mean, I probably could whip the Devil. Willie, is right; not because I am mean, it is because of God.

Some twenty plus years later; I reminded Willie about that conversation. I wanted him to understand that I am not that "vicious/crazy" person anymore. I wanted him to know; that I had not been in any physical combat in years and that I had learned with God's help, how to control myself and to do *so;* I had to be careful about the company that I kept. Willie looked at me; then he said; "that is only because no one has pissed you off." Wow! The more I tried to explained he could. not believe; that I am capable of not going to the extremeness and I had to; wrestled with those words of Willie's. For years, his statement was true, I had not been that (pissed off), however, I have been angry.

Again, God has given us all free will; with that in mind, I can choose my reactions at any giving time to any situation, do I call on God for help at the moment of a possible explosion? Most times when I choose to seek God's face first; I can fill his presents and I stop and thank the Lord for his presents; however, "free well;" have I let me decide what to do; on any given situation? Yes, and at that moment; I can still fill God's present telling me to back off, but "free will" I have chosen to be disobedient to God' s voice and do me. Now; with that being said, Queen B. Dye's spankings, or no match to God's. Now, I am dealing with a Higher Power a spiritual being and his spirt is searching; for my spiritual self and it is painful; we have a disconnect. My heavenly father is so Holly and my spirt is off track, due to my disobedient "free will." Now, how do I get back on track, by asking God for forgiveness and God forgives me quicker than I forgive myself; therefore, I use my "free will" most of the time righteously; I do not like the shame, nor a dampened spirt.

What I have learned is; that angrier is a normal human emotion. (Ephesians 4:26) Being angry is not the sin; it is the action taken because we are angry. Angrier is used by Satan as a demon; to control and destroy us; no different than any other demon and that demon has plagued me for a long time; but knowing that now; it is to my advantaged because I have been given the power to control the angry and not allow the angry to control me; but only if I chose to. Free will. In Galatians 5:22-23, when the Holy Spirt lives in us; we will produce the fruit of love, joy, peace, patience, kindness, goodness, faithfulness, gentleness, and self-control. I must say, I have notice whenever, I have allowed God to live in my life; I was better off and even when I did not allow God to live in my life; I could still see him in my mist.

I have been writing, revising and gathering my thoughts on Willie and I for about six weeks now. This day October 8ᵗʰ,201 6; I started writing again about 11am until around 5pm. I knew what I had shared up to this point was then; now I must write about the now of us. My mind was racing with thoughts; on how am I going to explain, why and how have we have not talked in five years now. After my mind settled down it was clear, nothing should change in my heart to write my truth; because again; "the truth is." What happened?

Willie, owned a second car a 1993 Toyota Corolla DX, that had been just sitting; he really did not have any use for the car and I did not have a car. He told me that the car had some problems but I could have that car; his only request was when I got the car running good; I would drive him to our birth place; Carrollton Georgia and I agree to do so; not saying when; nor would that be my first road trip. After several months of repairs; some tires, anew radiator, alternator, oil change and maybe a few other things; I believed that the car was road ready. I had missed some of my friends and the city lights of Cincinnati, Ohio. When I returned to Murphy Evon told me that he was mad; because I was supposed to have taken him to Georgia. I told Evon, yes, I did tell Willie that; I did not say when and I did not know his trip had to be first. I called him and told him the same thing and that we could go the next weekend; he refused. I saw him a few weeks later and I asked him again; he refused. Alright with me I have done all I could do; I am done.

I stayed in Murphy about year after his fallout with me and moved back to Cincinnati; we did not see each other or talked for several years at first. Then Evon began to tell me your brother asked about you (Willie) and then I had gone to Murphy as I pulled up into Evon's driveway; Willie was leaving; we just waved at one another not saying a word. Then maybe a year later my daughter had been in Murphy and she saw her uncle Willie and scolded him; on how could you still be mad at my mama and reminded him of how short life is and how we are few and this must stop. Mallari had called me about their conversation and that Willie had told her, he loves you; then she asked me what are you going to do? I reply to her; I am not going to do nothing. I told her what she did not know. She did not know before Evon had told me that he had asked about me; I had called him several times and he told Evon to tell me to lose his phone number and I did. She did not know six months prior to their conversation; he had told Evon to give me his phone number and I had tried to call him and sent him a text message without him responding. I then told my daughter Mallari; I am not worried about Willie and me, I love him, however I am going to leave us in God's hands to handle and God did.

Now, this is why I mentioned the date of October 8th, 2015; I had stopped writing for several hours when I received a phone call from my brother Willie at 8:16pm this day. We talked for a while; he said I wanted you to know that, I do love you and I want to hear you say you love me too and I did. I began to cry on the phone telling him that I had been writing and thinking about him all day and how amazing it was for me that God had felt my pain and heard my pied and soften your heart enough to call me. He first told me to stop crying, then he said you are lying. Then I asked him; why would I tell a lie on God? He hurried up to get off that thought. When we were finished talking; we told each other we love each other and he asked me to pray for him and I did, I do and I always will. I did not know how this part of my book would end; that is about Willie and me, but this seems like a good time. Hallelujah!

His love for me lasted, for two-months. To me Willie is like Pharaoh. They both are ignorant; as far as Pharaoh goes It took ten plagues; before he let the Hebrews go. It has taken me a life time to get my brother's love. They both have hard hearts and think they are the greater than God. What Happened?

My daughter was going through somethings; so, I packed up and moved back to Carrollton, where she was living for six-months. The time frame was November, 2015 until March, 2016. In December, I was at family home playing cards. (spades) He called me and he is drunk. I am talking to him, playing cards and talking trash to my opponents all at the same time. He becomes outraged saying is that all you do is play cards; no but at this moment yes. He wanted me to stop playing and give him all my attention. No; he started cussing me out and told me he hated me and that; he would never talk to me again, that was December, 2015 now, this May, 2020 and we have not spoken since. However; I sleep good at night and I am not depressed in the day. I do not have the energy for that foolishness. Again, I will continue to pray for him. I pray he changes his Pharaoh's ways; because he is standing face to face with God and God ask him; who do you think you are and why have you hated your sister?

ERVIN BROWN

ERVIN, IS THE youngest son of our mama. He was shy, a loner, meek, and sneaky. He too was a mama's boy. He was always humble and welled mannered toward to her. Anytime, she called out his name; he would always say, "mam." Ervin, would go to her immediately and say, "mam," his second word was, okay. Ervin, was never a big talker and he is still not; I wish he would talk? Yes, he has associate and have had others; to talk with. He has always made conversations quick and short.

Ervin, graduated from Murphy High School in 1976 and attended Brea College. He to was very athletic; playing basketball, and giving assistance to the players and coaches during football seasons; he played softball with the community league for years and he coached the community little league sports teams. Ervin and his wife Mattie-Ann-Allen-Brown has been married for over Thirty-five years and have three children Kayla, Christoper, Ashley and two grandchildren.

Ervin is not an alcoholic; however, he too has had some dealings with drugs. One day while talking with his sister-in-law; Zula-Mae Allen; when she said to me, Ervin started changing after our mother passed. Again, that was only conformation, of our love; for our mother and how she was our everything; her, loss has been very hard for us all; which is to say Ervin's hidden pain and in his quietness; having no one to share his sorrows with; however, he would have talked to mama. Although; I am, so thankful; that he stills attends the community church. Whenever; I go home to the South, visiting family; I reassure him staying in the church will strengthen any weakness and maintain spiritual stability.

Now; what was it like in the Brown's home between Ervin and I. Ervin, Evon and I did play a lot together and our mother wanted him to be out and about with, her two girls. Playing games such as tag, kickball, marble, riding bikes, making bows and arrow, red light green light and playing on a rug. What? Yes, we were probably around seven and nine; I would get on the rug and he would pull me from the living room; down the hall and back again. Then, we would switch place, playing for a least an hour. One night I quit, without giving him, his last given ride. He was mad about it. I did not care, then he got slick on me saying; that's okay; he still wanted to play and he would just pull me. I stepped on the rug, before I sit down, he snatches the rug out from under me; I fell face first busting my chin. I still have the scar. It was not that serious of a wound; I am bleeding and streaming blood murder; mama's is at home with guess in the kitchen and we are doing what we; do best acting out. She cleans me and the floor up and spanked Ervin.

Our Aunt Kathrine moved to Murphy; I guess around 1967, with her three youngest children's, and they moved in our old house in the holler; for a while. Ervin and I went together, to play with our cousins. On our way back, Ervin slipped on the dirty road, falling off the embankment into Miss Mattie Belle" yard, where her chicken coop was. Those chickens went wild; the chicken began to flock, fly and peck all over Ervin; pecking his head and snatch patches of his hair. He streaming, trying to fight them off, I am just standing there being in shock. Then; I'm like hell no, I'm going to kill them chicken. I grab a stick from the side of the road, jumped off the bank and started killing chickens with that stick. I grab him up; we held hands, walked up the bank and looked back, at the dead chickens, blood and feathers everywhere. When we got home and told our mama all about it, she doctored on Ervin; then she said to me; "so; you were in shock;" "I replied, I was in shock." She said, "no such a word;" if your brother or sister is in danger; you jump right in immediately," and that is how we lived it.

As for, Jerry it was cars; Ervin was animals and insects. One day he and I was playing kickball on side of the house, the score was about even, then he starts kicking nothing but homeruns; that's when the ball goes up on the bank. I got tired of going to get the ball and told him if he kicks another, I'm not going to go get it. He kicks another, I sit down on the ground, he ran his homerun, then went to retrieve the ball; he stepped on a bee's nest. He is running off the bank with the ball in his hand streaming. I jump up asking what's wrong, then I see bees coming out of his shirt and he is slapping at his legs. I'm tearing off his shirt and telling him to pull off his pants, he did; we ran into the house putting alcohol all over him, he survived that too.

Since I have been talking about my family private life, the love and the craziness of fights. If you are wondering if Ervin and I ever had a fight, yes; we had two, he won one and I stole one. To be completely honesty, the fight Ervin won, I really cannot remember how it got started but knowing me, I started it. I can only speculate. Maybe, I had something of his and would not give it back, or ate up his cookies, or just being an ass, thinking he would not bother me. I had no idea that this sweet, submissive, quite boy could even fight. If memory serves me right, we were arguing and I got off the first and only lick. That is probably why I do not remember many details, accept we fought and I lost.

The day I stole the win, one of my friends, Ervin and I were in the kitchen. We were hungry and assessing; what's available good to eat. Most likely leftovers since I had a fork; not the normal bologna sandwich, with chips and grape Kool-Aid, which was very popular at the Brown's. We were at the table eating our food, when Ervin started being nasty, chewing up his food and opened his mouth to show-off the chewed-up food in his mouth. I asked him kindly to stop being nasty, he continues; I told him that was not funny; he ignored me. Then all of a sudden; I stabbed him in the jaw with my fork, leaving the fork behind. He reached, pulled the fork out of his jaw and four little blood spots were oozing out of his jaw. My thoughts were oops; he is going to beat me up. I took off running into the bathroom because that was the only room in the house that would lock. However, you could unlock it with a butter knife and he was trying to unlock the door. I kept my hand on the lock for dear life and resting my hand when, he would walk off but hold the lock again when I heard him returned. I stayed in the bathroom for two hours; until our mother got home to save me. That was another top five whipping I got; however; I thought it would have been better, then the one Ervin wanted to give me. I truly believe, we never had another fight was because we knew each other; I could not win knuckle- up and he could not trust what, I may do and then again, I loved my baby brother and did not want to fight with him.

However, I was always ready to defend him though.

I used the last sentence just to set up this incident. At this time, I must have been around eleven and Ervin would have been about thirteen. I cannot remember, if the old school house was there or the new community center was there; which does not really matter it is the same land. If you are coming up Texana road, then you will make a right; to go up a deep short hill; to the building but when you turn immediately there *is* an old big tree, that's been there for years and is still there today. That is where Ervin was along with probably about ten grown community men and the men were drinking. Knowing my brother Ervin, he would have never been in their mist; unless someone called out to him to come.

Remember me talking about the afro hair style, Ervin had one too, however; Ervin was not concerned about his hair everyday like Willie, their age different was the different. Now, I was all the way at the top on the back side, of the building, playing with other community children. Then we could hear some commotion going on, like screaming, loud voices and laughter, so; we went to investigate the situation. What I saw angry me and hurt me so badly. Two of the men were holding Ervin and one was combing his hair and the others were laughing. I ran up to them, first trying to free him, they are pushing me back then I tried to take the comb; all failed. Not; giving up I started picking up rocks, zooming them so fast and hard; that sparks were created by hitting other rocks on the ground and the tree. They let him go and they all dispersed because I was still throwing rocks and cursing like a sailor. We went home; we kept it secret because; I was sort worried about all the cussing I had done; I did not want to tell that part.

This incident was just a day and a time. Believe me when I say, this could not and would not happen today in Texana. The number one reason is "no one," is that crazy to touch any bodies kids, nor be that drunk; drugged out or retarded. The ratification would be swift and horrific. Back in the day they meant; no harm I guess, they saw it as fun, no such thing then and really not today. Also, the state frown on such action as child abuse.

Growing older but not grown. One late night my friend Renee, her boyfriend a white guy his name is Scott out of Haysville North Carolina and his best friend a black guy named mike. I think Scott's came from a well to do family, Scott drove a new; two toned Camaro dark brown and light brown. We were all friends. I must have been about fourteen and Ervin would had been sixteen. One night the five of us were together; like many times, we are riding around in Texana. I guess we got bored, driving up and down the road; Ervin was doing the driving, mike is up front Scott, Renee and I are in the back. We plotted up and agreed to leave the safety of the hill. (Texana) At the bottom of the hill, we are at the stop sign; keep straight was not a good idea, going toward town. So, making the left, onto this curve road called Joe Brown Highway, was the best option because at the end of that road a quick left; we would be back in Texana. Half way around the road, the cops blue-lighted us, was the only one that had license; in a panic; they decided to switch drivers. Mike, moved to the back first, then Scott got mike seat, then Scott and Ervin switch seat; wild crazy children. After the switch, Scott pulled over, the officer asked for his license and registration. We are as quite as a mouse, thinking we are good. The officer asks have we being drinking or is there drugs in the car; "no we all replied;) so you want mind if we search the car; then we were all asked to get out of the car. After the search, no drugs and no smell of alcohol nor empty cans; the officer said; "I saw you two switching drivers. We all started singing at the same time; "no he was driving." The officer being to tell us he could take every one of us to jail; so, do not lie again. Ervin admitted; he was driving; Renee and I are crying. Then the officer warned us how dangerous that was to switch driver and, on this road, especially you all could have been killed, however; I know you are just being "dumb kids;" and your plus; no drugs; nor alcohol, good kids. The officer told Scott to take us home; for Scott to, go home too and do not let him see us again. What a nice offer, our mother would have been crushed, most like not a whipping though, but a long hard punishment.

Again, we are who we are; however, who we are can be misconstrue, by others. As mention before, Ervin, has always being quiet, shy or just not a big conversationalist, which confused two of my children. I had come home to Murphy to visit my family. I went over to my ex-home to see my children; they were like thirteen and ten, when they said to me; they do not think uncle Ervin love them. What? Why? He never talks to us, when he sees us. So; I assured them, that' just his personality; he never talked much to me either when, we were growing up. Then, they told me about a ball game and uncle Ervin gave some other children a ride and did not ask them. Okay; he probably knew your daddy is coming to pick both of you up. Then, my ex spoke up and said something; of course; he is on his children team. I really do not know what my ex said because, I cut him off midway. I said to them; again, that's is just Ervin and there is nothing anyone can ever say; to convince me, that my brother does not love my children. Later on, that night there was a community party. Ervin was there, so I told him what they had said. He looked at me, so shocked and hurt; so, I told him please, when you see them again strike up a conversation with them; he did and that's been over twenty years ago, they love him; he loves them and they know it is so.

Ervin and I has always been sort of distance, not because of the lack of love but personality, and that's okay. Again, somethings are best unsaid because without details, he has come to my rescue too. Not only is he my brother, he is my friend.

EVON T. JOHNSON

MY SISTER, EVON is truly the love of my life and yes; she feels the same way about me. She has always been my best friend and always on my side. Growing up Evon was quiet, sort shy and sneaky; like Ervin; not friendly; and a bit hateful like Irma Jean. I could always tell, when Evon was getting angry because her eyes would take on a slant; like Chinese eyes; seriously, I first notice the eyes many years ago; especially when I would tease her; calling her "scaredy-cat." Being so mild mannered, she was often picked on by other children. There were times, I had wished, I could had been able to balance us, by trading some of her mildest, with some of my meanest; however, I am glad that there was no such magic; therefore, we could just be ourselves. We did what most sisters did, I guess; we shared clothes, secrets, some friends, toys, bedroom, food·, basically everything but boyfriends.

Evon, graduated from Murphy, High School and 1977. The only sport, she participates in, was softball and she was a good first- base-woman. However; she loves sports a big fan of college ball and professional ball. Shortly after school, she married James Johnson; whom most call him "zeke;" I call him, "papa or brother-in-law and he calls me sis." They just recently celebrated forty years of marriage. I am so proud of them; they kept the promise; of better or worse and for years now; they have treated each other; like the king and queen they are. They have two children Crystal, Devon and six grandchildren.

I'm grateful that Evon is not an alcoholic, nor drug addict and she has never smoked cigarettes.

That's not to say, she has never had a drink or two; nor hit a joint passing by. Especially, being part of a long line of a co-dependency family member and growing up in a community; where drinking alcohol and smoking weed was sociable accepted it' a wonder. Evon and I are only seventeen months apart; we were together a lot, or at least nearby.

I know by now; you the reader is probably wondering, with all that spoken love, when was the fight? Never. We, have never in our life hit one another; however, there was once a pushing fight training exercise.

It was a hot summer day; I am sitting *on* our front porch; anticipating a cool breeze. As I was sitting there, I could hear some commotion, from down the street; my thoughts where I did not care it was hot, so whoever or whatever it was about, it was not my concern. As they got closer, I could hear someone say, "hit her again, another said, I will push her to you," still, I just sit there. Then when they got closer into my view, I was still unsure what was up; until they got even to our mail box. I went into a complete rage. Some community girls were instigating another girl to hit and push Evon. It's hot, I had been hearing this nonsense for at least fifteen minutes; now I see. I jump up, mama had a pretty rose bush tided up with a string around a stick. *I* snatch out the stick, ran to the road and it was all over. I was cussing and swinging that stick; hitting them; they started running up the hill and I follow suit, chasing them around the curve. When *I* got back to the house, *I* threw the stick on the porch and went into the kitchen, where Evon was, getting herself something to eat. I started on her, snatching her food from her and telling her it is time for her to learn how to fight, Then, I started pushing her, she is crying and telling me to leave her along. No, I want leave you alone; my heart was hurting all at the same time for her.

Bless her little heart, she had already been terrorized all the way home; now I am doing the same thing. However; it was for her good; so, I pushed her again and again and again; then it happens, she pushed me so hard that I felled backwards against the back door and the whole window shattered, literally, I do not know why I did not get cut, I guess God was on my side because, my heart was in the right place.

We, just looked at each other and the window; then I said, "see you can fight." That incident builds up her courage, there were; no more need for anymore fight lessons and over the years, she has won many battles. I tied the roses back around the stick and cannot remember the lie we told mama about the window; however, mama had the maintenance man to fix the window the next day.

This is a story about back in the day, when a two-parents, working family; they had cars, owned there home and had four children. It has always been a good thing to be connected with people that had means. Their oldest son liked the girls and the girls liked him. This boy dressed well, his hair was always neat, he was welled mannered an all-around good guy. I liked him and was cool with the Idea, of him liking my sister. He came to the house, once or twice a week, for several weeks. One night I was out in about, when I saw this white girl pick him up; I thought what's that's about? A few hours later, I am still out and I see the girl bring him back; to the same spot he, then kisses her good-by. I went home after that; Evon was at home, I never said a word to her about what I had seen. Within an hour, the boy is knocking on the door; who is it; I asked, when he answered, I opened the door. I let him have it. I told them both at the same time all I had seen, then of course; I threw out some of the most vulgarity words every and told him to get *off* our porch and do not come back, however, he did come back over the years to see Willie. He and I are friends, we have been friends for years, I love him very much and when he sees me; he will sometimes bring up that night and a jokingly manner and we laughs about it; he knew he was wrong.

Another memorable story, one night, Evon, my friend Sharon and I was going to this teenager's party; the building was rented out, the old community Juke-Joint spot. Sharon comes to our house to get dressed, the time is about seven O'clock and we decided to drink some of pops moonshine; that was in the kitchen pantry on the shelf; just to get our little buzz on before, we got there. Evon and Sharon stopped drinking, I kept drinking, they warned me to stop and reminded me; that my pops was going to know someone has been in his quart jar. My crazy thought was, I will pour me another drank and add water to the moonshine and I did. Now, I am drunk, sick, hot and spinning as if I was on a merry-go round. Holding on to the kitchen table, I made it to the back door, opening the door and laid on the back porch. I awoke, when I heard Evon and Sharon voices, when I was able to get up, opening the back door, I enter and I told them, I was ready now to go. Go where, the party is over, they had been and back. What? The time now is four AM in the morning, our talking woke up mama, she did not know I was on the back porch, she thought; we had just come in. I missed the party; my pops asked who put the water in his quart jar and of course I did not know anything about it. I learned early own that, I was not a drinker; yes, I still have had a drank at times but never like that again.

December, 1st, 2014 Evon had a heart attack, I prayed and prayed that the Lord would keep her and he did, I went home to be supported as well as to be supportive; for Zeke and the children. I stay a couple of weeks before returning to Cincinnati. Jesus! It happened again, she had another heart attack; on January, 30th, 2015 back to back. Wow! I am devastated, scared, crying and unable to pray and that's okay. Romans 8: 26-27, the scripture reads that, the Holy Spirit, intercedes for us (God's children) through wordless groans. In other word the Spirit prayed for me; yes, Lord. Then I began to call on my prayer warriors at my church. James: 5 vs-16 reads that, the prayers of the righteous availeth much. In other words; when God's children pray, He hears their petitions, that we desire of Him. God is good I praise him every day, for his kindness and mercy. However, do not get this wrong, we all are going to die and all prayer are not, answered the way we want, our prayers or prayers basted on his Will, because his Will, will be done. I am thankful, she was in His Will and has been okay now for five years,

God is good. As I continue to write understand this, someone once said. "What has already been revealed, has already been redeemed.)

My Town Murphy

MURPHY, IS PROBABLY no different than any other small rural town. Where everybody, knows everybody. Being raised in the mountain of North Carolina has been a blessing for us all. This is where we learned the greatest values of life. Such as faith respect, forgiveness, love, friendships, sacrifices and dependency. Which; that is not to say everything was always Lilly white. I cannot remember everything that happen, but I do remember when the black children were not allowed to swim in the town pool.

Now, I do not know if it was county owned but I know, "up town community white men", The Lion Club operated it the pool." I think I was about eleven or twelve, when black children were aloud to swim there. I also remember, when Black people had to sit upstairs in the balcony to see a movie; not aloud on the first floor except to buy snacks. Then, there was the time the Klan came for a rally. However, these things were over thirty to fifty years ago.

As a child I can remember the county's politic. The older Texana community folks, loving, to vote on county's politic because back in the day it was money in it. Texana folks did not have any money, the white Politian's had the money but the people of Texana could make some money. Those with cars would drive the community folks to vote and was paid to do so. However, they had another "top secret," job which was to persuade the voter to vote a certain way a democratic vote would get a pint of moonshine and twenty-five dollars and a republican vote was a pint of real liquor, meaning manufactory made and forty dollars. Everyone in the community did not know the secret or they were to high class to participate in it. With all of that being said the people were going to vote their way anyways, they probably lied at times; for the higher pay. By time I got old enough to vote, that system was long gone. However; todays elections or rigged in some shape form or fashion even today except on a wider scale; not about the American Citizens but whom, those with the money wants. This next statement, I will make, some will not believe me and I care less; again, truth is. When I vote in the 2016 election after making my selection; just as I went to pull the lever, I notice the check was for Trump; no way I would have done that, therefore you can think; that, I had made a mistake, no the machine were being interfered with, so how many people missed the switch?

As for recreations, we had a game room, a hamburger shop, driving in theater, driving up and down in town, house parties, skating, community sports, four wheeling in the mountains, parking and smoking weed. Then, there were the structured programs, such as the brownie, girls/boys scout, Four-H, the dance teams of mountain Clogging, Red cross fundraising and sleep overs and I participate in it all.

Murphy, is a great little town, I love to go home to visit and will probably move back there one day if God is willing. Believe me when I say there is plenty of old and new money there and the perfect areas to make some money; the town has grown so much. Murphy has many denominations of churches, restaurants, banks/credit union, convention stores, grocery stores, land for homes/business/farming, golf course, casino, bars, hotels, community college, a growing hospital, manufactories, parks, camping ground, lakes/rivers, nice venue, the Fields of the woods a Bible park, gyms, salons and mini shopping centers. In there is more, I just mention a few things and I must say, some of, the things I mention was not even there when I lived there; it is growing, but for most it is the people; although, I will share some shameful stories of a few as I continue to write; however, they do not represent my town Murphy. Murphy is located in an area, whereas, we are two hours at most, from Atlanta, Chattanooga, Gatlinburg Tennessee, Asheville, Greenville, South Carolina, Knoxville, and Cherokee the Indian Reservation.

My town Murphy is a place where love is real and help; from many directions are available. Not only the County's systems but outreach groups such as the Reach Program, for battered women and children, animal shelter, food pantry and the communities are always willing to assist in fundraising, for someone in need and of course, I am sure there are more of such. Even with all of that, there are the individuals, whom will help you if you are hungry, need a place to sleep, in need of money, a job and if they are unable to help you, they know someone who can. This I know because, I have been in the need before as well as being the giver. Not only me but others; in Murphy and Texana that, have developed friendships; that has lasted since childhood. One of the most important things for me in writing my story is that, "what ever I say, them that matters to me and I matter to them, want mind and them that minds, do not matter"

ME MYSELF AND I

To be totally honest, as I look back over my life; I realized, about fifteen years ago; that these three persons are real. I cannot remember the circumstance; of why my friend Renee and I was having a conversation, to why; I would have said, I do not need anybody, all I need is me, myself and I. What a dumb statement, we all need somebody, sometimes. However, this is not about the needs of others; nor the corrective way to use them and the English Language, but who we are as these three individual persons. This is what "I" have learned about me. Me is the worst of all, me is capable of much, me is self-centered, me is making something right when wrong and as you continue to read my story; you will see "me" a lot. Now, "I" on the other hand is a little better than "me." "I" can change my mind on a dime, I want what I want, I cannot be persuaded; in trying to do so, "me" shows up, I am for what, I think is right and I do not have any problems, of telling anybody to their face, about themselves, because truth is. "Myself" is not myself it is really, just "self." So, who is self? Self is a spirit, whether it is a good spirit or an evil spirit. We are spiritual beings in a natural form and it is up to us to tap into, that spirit; our real "self." Self is really who God deigned us to be. (Romans:12) Be you transformed; become a new person; by first changing the way we think. Starting with self-checking, stop pretending, stop being conceited and stop false love; this is only a start. Even though, living my life as "self," me and I are still real, self has to battle with them many days; however, now self-wins most of the time.

When I entered, the first grade at Murphy Elementary School in the fall of 1966, for the most, North Carolina's Schools were no longer segregated. However, history slates this battle started in 1954, with Brown vs Board of Education, the case went all the way, to the Supreme Court, which ruled that segregation was unconstitutional. Still, taking until 1960 before the first black student was enrolled in the state capitol of Raleigh, North Carolina and it took between, 1971and 1972 before North Carolina actual met all the requirement of the Supreme Courts. Therefore; that, history alone had to have been some racial tension; simply the timing; however, I do not remember much about my first four years of school; therefore, it must have been good.

My fifth-grade year was an absolute horror, the fear of this one particular day, I can still see me in that moment and feeling the same fear. My homeroom teacher, name was Shelia Tate. This was her first year and last year at Murphy Elementary. She had come from Robersonville, North Carolina approximately; forty-five minutes from Murphy. Robersonville are Indians and white people; however, times have changed and there are a few Blacks, that lives there; our schools played against Robersonville in sports and we went there for, school field trips, to a park called Joyce Kilmer, with trees, that took ten children holding hands to reach around the trees. Miss Tate, was a young white woman and she had probably had not been in the presents of "Black people," at least this close and personal?

Now, she has a Black child to teach. Miss Tate did not like me from the start. I can only ponder why, maybe because I was Black or maybe I was not the child, she had imagined what a Black child was. I was sweet, funny, happy, smart and a clean little girl. Every day she would stand over me at my desk and eat butterfingers candy bar and the crumbs would drop on my desk and me; plus singing; these same two songs; one was "Mary, Mary quite contrary how do your garden grow? With silver bells, and cockle shells, and pretty maids all in a row." The other song was, "Mary had a little Lamb, little Lamb, little Lamb, his fleece was white as snow and everywhere; that, Mary went the Lamb was sure to go." I hated those songs and I really do not like them now. She always wore dresses and her hair was always pinned up with many Bobbie-pins. At the end of each school day, there would be two bells. The first bell would be for the first group of students to leave. I left on the second bell; however, this particular day is girls scout day and Evon is leaving on the first bell. I had fifty- cents; in dimes, nickels and pennies. I paused for a minute, when the first bell sounded, to give Evon time to be close. Not; wanting to miss her, I got up out of my seat, stood in the door, waiting on Evon to come. Miss Tate instructed me to return to my seat; I asked her to let me give my sister my money; so, she can bring me some candy home. No, she replied, then I begged her please Miss Tate; I can see her, she is almost here. Miss Tate got up from her desk, came over to me grabbing and shaking me; so, force- fully I dropped my money. I could see my money rolling down the hall and the children are quickly picking it up. Then she dragged me back to my desk; shoved me into my seat, I jumped back up and she! shoved me back down and slapped my face.

Then, I had these thoughts; this bitch has been nothing but mean to me, singing in my ears, smacking and dripping candy on me, she has caused me to lose my money and now she is beating me up. This is where, I went blank; however, I had to have jumped back up, push- ing her against the chalk board, pulling all of her hair-pins out, of her hair and hitting her in the face. I did not realize what had, happen until, I heard her screaming, by the streams I knew somethings was not right. I stopped and when I looked at her and my surrounding, it was a hot mess. Now; her hair is down going every direction, there are claw marks and red spots all in her face; plus, hair pins are all in the floor. My thoughts went to I am in danger, the school principal, Mr. Bill Hughes is going to paddle me. I took off running and hid outside against a little cut out against the school building. I was shaking and praying, that the bus would not be late. The buses always line up the same way every day and my bus number forty-six was always first.

When I saw the bus top the hill, I ran to the bus stop, when the bus driver opened the door, I got on the bus and hid in the back on the floor. The bus driver name is Phil Blackwell, his parents, were friends to my parents as a matter of fact, his dad, Felix Blackwell is who moved us to Murphy. When the other children got on the bus, those up front did not know, I was on the bus. Those who did was my friends or knew there would be repercussion, if they squealed on me. Mr. Hughes got on the bus; I could hear in his voice; he wanted to beat my butt. He was asking the children had anyone seen me; not one said a word. As we were driving off, I got up off the floor, looking out the window, Mr. Hughes was scanning, the school yard, still looking for me. Then Phil asked me, "Mary what have you done." I told him, "I beat-up my teacher," he laughs. Immediately, when I walked into our house, I called my mother at work hysterical. Telling her, Mr. Hughes is going to paddle me and the white people are coming to kill me. I was so neurotic, Mrs. Louise had to bring my mama home. I am crying as I tells mama what has been going on and what had happened, she embraced me and with an infallible tone, of her words, I knew I was safe. The next morning my mother and I walked to school together. I was removed out of Miss Tate's homeroom; I repeated the fifth grade and Miss Tate left the school at the end of the year. Now, this is not to say; these changes were a direct cause of the incident, only the assumption it had to have had some influence.

Being set back, I had a new set of friends and this is when, I started participating in all the school and county's programs. Just as teachers has favorite, students have favorite, for me there were three. Mrs. Marie Hendrix, her daughter- in-law Mrs. Brenda Hendrix and Mrs. Ida Town son. Mrs. Marie a elder lady with a kindred soul, she loved all the children. Not only was her hugs and kisses being sweet, she scolded sweetly. However, you knew you were being scolded; by a steady pull of your ear. Mrs. Brenda Hendrix a beautiful and elegance lady, she could inspire any little girl to keep herself up. Yet, it was her teaching skills, that made you want to learn and she made you learn. It is because of her; I can count in my head with accuracy or estimate within a narrow margin. She used a program; of a count of thirty problems per-sheet, addition, subtraction, multiplication and division and you had one minute to complete. Every day you were giving a new sheet; however, if you missed one, you had to do that one an again, one-hundred was a must to go to the next level. Miss Ida Townson was the teacher that went over and beyond a teacher's duties. Renee and I spent many nights at Mrs. Townson's home, eating at her table, playing with her children and receiving gifts. Her son Eric had a safe with his money in it, Renee and I tried to con him out of some of the money, he would not do it; however, we kept asking, then he said if you can figure out the combination, you can have some. What did he say that for?

Renee and I sit up all night trying to open up the safe, while in Renee's hands the safe popped open. We got us some of the money; not all, then closing the safe back, that was the bet.

I entered Murphy Junior High in the fall of 1973; with enthusiasm of being in "Jr. High," riding the high school bus and knowing, I was only a side-walk away from the high school. And anticipation of pep rallies, bonfires, school dances, high school "boy," and no more looking at first graders. However, it was not long to realize some, of the same issues arises; just a different place, adjusting to new rules, teachers and student. Murphy is the center of other communities and out of these communities are other schools. Now, these other school such as Martin Creek, Peachtree, Ranger, Hanging Dog and white Church; only goes to the sixth grade, so many of those students came to Murphy, junior high.

Keep in mind; that, this is the early seventy and most of these students had never talked, played, ate, sit by; nor walked; with any black children before. Needless to say, there were plenty of negativity warranted, to misunderstanding and misinformation, from both sides of this blending together. Characteristically, of me, I have never faced change; without, some sort of episode. However, I am going to jump ship at this point, to go in another direction of my life, then we will return to the seventh grade.

I just thought this would be a good time, to talk about other things, in the Brown's household; When we were growing up, to shine the light on other things about me. I can cook. I started cooking at the age of eleven, I was always in the kitchen, helping mama cook and asking question, early on. I did a lot of the cooking growing up; so, as my mother would not have to, after a hard day of work. I can remember the, government commodity foods, powder milk, canned lunchmeat, (spam like) raisins, canned fruit, a whole pre-cooked chicken in a can, canned stew, canned juices, powder eggs, canned vegetable and the best blocked cheese in the world. I would always put the food up, and packed a few of the items into a box to hide, so when, the food was low, I would pull it out. We all had chores, the boys took out the garbage, cut the grass and kept their room up. Evon in I had to rotate, washing the dishes nightly, kept our room up and the living room cleaned. We were all like mama as for as work ethics. My first summer job was, with the Unite States Forrest Service. Every summer we worked, Evon and I both worked at the County's Recreation Department, I also worked at the County's Court House in the Mapping Department and the County's Library. We all had fairly longevity with our jobs, anywhere between three and twenty-five years.

Although; I had many friends, Renee and I was together the most; we were everywhere and doing much. Rather, we were getting cute to go to the County's Fair, or in the car with our little league basketball coach, Peggy Wells listen to; Frankie Valli and the Four Seasons, singing "Sherry Baby" and raking leaves in the fall for, this old lady; once I dropped my paid in her yard and she was sweet enough to bring it right back to me. Renee and I was just a bit mischievous at times. Sneaking up on the drunks, that was at her mother's house, to see what they were doing and clip money off of them. One day this old drunk man, his name was, Harlan Kincaid was lying in the yard. We were trying to stand him up to check his pockets and he knew; drunk, swaying backward and forward; he points his finger at us and said these words, "aah little children, I would never tell you anything wrong." What? However, I changed my mind and helped him sit on the porch. Those words of this drunk man stay in my mind; of what he said and I have lived my life that way as I got older and understood them even more. Do not encourage anyone to do wrong. This story, I have just shared actually goes deeper then; that, this man came up in a Christian family of the Texana community, his father was a Deacon, his uncle was a Deacon, his brother was a preacher and cousins of Gospel Singers. What happen to him? I do not know; however, when this man died, he had walked, to the church it was no services going on that day, he went there and laid on the church porch and then, he died. Isaiah 53:6, he went back home at the end.

Renee and her sister Teresa, being raised by their grandmother Miss Louise. (Mama lse) Teresa was always the; "good girl" however, not perfect, no one is; we all got saved when; we, were around ten or eleven; however, Renee and I did church and the streets too. Teresa lived a teenager's life but never did, as Renee and I. Teresa has been a solider in the Lord's army for forty plus years, she too has written a book; on stepping out on faith, her pains, her victories and her life in Murphy, North Carolina, the book title: **The Journey Beyond Shallow Waters.**

Renee and I were always up to somethings, we use to play games with her grandmother and my mama. Although, we were allowed to spent the night, with each other many times, sometimes we were already instructed at times; no, sleep-over. This is the time, when we played out our game. I would stay at her house to late or visa- versa, then play scared to come home; please let me/her spend the night, it worked sometimes, sometimes not. This story is about a night the game was not working. Renee was at my house, mama lse told her no,

Renee is crying, she is scared, we had mama to call mama lse. Mama lse still said no and tell Renee to get home right now! Mama told mama lse, she would let me walk Renee home but I would need to stay the night, mama lse agreed. Another true story, as we were walking up the hill, side by side, Renee is on the left and I'm on the right, as we topped the hill into the curve; on the left, off the embankment, I saw a big glowing round object. I did not say a word and I did not know if she seen it or not. We kept on walking, then I looked again and it was rising, then I looked directly at Renee and she looked at me; I knew in her expression, she had seen it to; but we still did not say a word; we begun to walk a little faster. When, we looked again it was gone, from that spot and was behind us; we screamed and took off running. I looked back again; this, thing was in a bouncing, slow moving motion toward us but never touched the ground. Not, looking back again just running all the way to Renee's house. We were so tried and afraid; that, when we opened the door, we failed into the floor crying and trying to get our breath. There were others in the house, I just do not remember who though; an aunt or a cousin; however, mama lse asked us, "what is wrong with Yaw?" Trying to breath and answers the question, at the same time; finally, we speak and tell them what happen. Mama lse, told us that was nothing but "minerals" and the minerals was gravitating to the heat, of our bodies. "Bull-Crap," we went along, with her explanation, it sounded good, we needed to hear a simply justification and mama lse, being an older lady must know what, she is talking about. Well, I do not know what it was; however, I will make lite of; the experience now, if it was scanning us, it knew; we were not what it was looking for. Renee and I would had destroyed that ball, at least died trying.

After school, cleaning the house and doing my school homework; I would go to meet Renee at the building. Miss Al-Jane an older sweet lady in the community, had fruit trees in her yard; there were, apples, peaches, plums and pears. We, the children of the community were allowed to get the fruit; that was on the ground; however, Renee, I and others would try our luck; pulling, the fruit off the trees. Miss Al-Jane would catch us most of the time, coming to the door; to scold us; we would take off running. Ernest and Grace Sudderth, lived up above Miss Al-Jane and there were fruit trees; on the side of their house too. One day Renee and I went up to the Sudderth's to get some fruit. They had some mean dogs; that were chained up; however, not this day. Back in the day, we mostly; called dogs; just dogs; now, that I am looking back; I believe they were either bulldogs or rottweilers, anyways the dogs were big and vicious. As we were gathering fruit, we see the loose dogs, rushing our way. Renee and I ran, jumping on an old rotten chicken coop; pieces of the coop are falling off and our weight, is causing the coop to give-in. As; we, hit the ground Ernest, grabbed both dogs' collars, holding them tightly and pulling them back. The dogs were, still trying to get to us; up on their back legs, slobbering at the mouth, showing teeth and growling. I have never forgotten; that scene, I am afraid of dogs and I do not like dogs; therefore, I avoid dogs and they need to avoid me too. However; that incident, did not affect, Renee like that; she has three or four big dogs.

Again, as I keep looking back over my life and revealing more, I have noticed many things as far as my behaviors goes. On the normal, if no one bothered me or mind, I did not bother anyone. Also, I realized at times, I simply thought, I could get by with some of my mess. Then, there were times, I did behave or avoid trouble because of the fear of mama's discipline; however, there were the times, I was already caught-up; in, the moment and did not care. Thinking back I must have been nine or ten when, my mama said to me, "May-re, I just do not know, the more I punish, whip, talk and pray for you, you keep doing un-called for stuff, nothing seems to work." However, what she did not know; was her actions were working because, if not I would have probably been worse. Desperate to understand and to protect me from impending trouble, she seeks professional help, with a child's Psychologist, Dr. Peter Cook. I was seeing this doctor, maybe once a week for several months. I enjoyed my sessions.

Touching and playing with his things on his desk, as he asked me questions and I was more, then glad to answers them. Although; I cannot remember the question but knowing me, I answered them honestly and I'm sure this Doctor received an ear full. Then, the sessions seemed to have suddenly stopped or I suddenly realized that, I had not been there in a while. So, I asked why I have not seen the Doctor lately, she said; "the Doctor told her, that nothing was wrong with me, I was just mean and I would grow out of it." Really! Yes; I grew out of it forty-five years later. Now, I see it as just another adult that failed me.

Okay, let's go back to Junior High seventh grade; pastor, teacher, Mr. Marvin Hampton, the "man." I had Mr. Hampton as by reading teacher. He never disrespected a student; he did not allow, students to disrespected one another and most definitely do not even think about, disrespecting him. Mr. Hampton was serious and funny, if you knew him. If he caught you with chewing gum in your mouth during class; he would make you take it out of your mouth and stick it to your forehead, until class was out. We all knew that; however, we either forgot to take, the gum out or thought, we could get by, he caught someone probably once a week, I got caught too. Dumb children. Every punishment I, ever received from him was justify, hard but fair. The punishments were like, write a hundred times, I will not whatever, read an extra book, come sit in his room during your gym time; such things as that. In his reading class, he would read a chapter daily, testing periodically to see if you are listening. Sometimes, we choose our own book; Although; at times, we had to choose a book off of his book-list. Each student had a certain time to finish a book and had a calendar's date, to stand before the class and tell the story, of your book. Every book I read, Mr. Hampton, would say, "Mary you get an, "A" for comprehension and an, "A" for deliverance." Mr. Hampton is gone now too; however, what I really learned in this class, was to "pay close attention, to every little detail of everything."

By now you the reader has probably beginning to get an idea who I'm; that is if you have follow, with intense comprehended and I hope you have; however, when most people think I will react one way, I will react in a total different way; however, this story is not that one. You will see it coming. In my way of thinking, I could never envision, the notion two wrongs; not making it right. At least in this time frame of my life. I was a sensitive child and I could sense the vibes of whether you liked me or not and I was cool with that, because everybody is not going to like you and most definitely not love you. I always knew who was whom and I would never display myself; differently just to obtain, someone's dislike to like. That would have been a consciously waste of energy, you either got me or you did not. I could feel early on, the animosity toward me, from my physical education teacher, Mr. Melvin Payne, he too came from an area called Hiawassee Dam, that was really racist back in the day, I know the area is somewhat different now; yet, the area is still not for me. I could see the disfavor for me in his eyes, as well as in his voice. I dreaded his class, I was literally afraid of him, I also felt as he senses that and enjoyed my fear. This man was at least four feet's taller than me and every bit of hundred and twenty-five pounds heavier than me. One day while playing softball, I hit the ball close to the pitcher's mounds. Mr. Payne, position was hind-catcher. Granted I play softball, I know that a ball hit near the pitcher's mounds; most of the time the pitcher gets the ball and the hind-catcher, may have to in a crunch. Anyways, I'm running fast to first base and apparently, he is running fast to get to the ball. He throws the ball so hard hitting me in the small of my back, I had to stop and massage by back, for about a minute. During that minute, "me crazy" kicked in, he meant to it, this was no mishap, I was already on the base. The others came up, to me, asking was I okay; no, one had gone to get the ball, which had bounced off of me and rolled off to the right of the first base. At that very moment all fear of him disappeared. Calmly walking off, the base to retrieved the ball. I strolled, up to him and with all my strength; I threw the ball, hitting him in his chest. Naturally, he was in shock and so were the other children. I did not care and I was angry. I had already; planned in my head, if he touched me, I'm picking up the bat; then,

MARY & A-HALF

I told him into his face, that was no accident and what I did was not either. He ended the class early and my punishment was detention, for a couple of weeks, which was fine with me; I believed the means were justified and the clincher of this incident, I never got hit with the ball again and I no longer feared him.

Life, has taught me many things; like the saying goes, "experience is a good teacher," at least it should be. What I have learned about most people; they, cannot stand the truth. Serious! Why is that? I will tell you why, first of all they have to hear it and deep down; they, know it is so; however, they still do not want to accept because, they have to look at themselves in the wrong. They are angry; that, you see the truth and bold enough to speak, the truth. "Truth speaking" and boldness; makes enemy. Follow this next story very closes and you too will see clearly; my, philosophy of, dislike for truth.

Earlier I had shared about the mixing of other county's schools and the different cultures blending. Unknown to me, why this boy name, chuck and I did not like each other, from day one. He is looking at me, with a belligerently attitude and I'm returning, the same message. I'm not sure exactly, where chuck came from, I believe, his family had come from Florida; so not sure, if directly from or from one of the other schools; not that it matters. The looks finally escalated into an argument and he calls me the "N" word. I wanted to punch him in his eye. Instead, I decide just to tell on him, get him into trouble and I dodge the bullet of trouble. When I went to coach Watson about the situation, he was unconcerned, he did not say a word; just looked at me like I was the villain. Now, I'm hurt and angry; which is a dangerous combination for me. My mine has jumped off the, track wanting to explode; due to this, disappointment. Junior high students ate lunch in the high school cafeteria, when I saw Evon, I told her what Chuck had said and how I felt, coach Watson did not care. Telling Evon coach was not going to do anything about it. The coach overheard me talking to my sister. After returning from lunch, I was in class and coach came to get me and Chuck was with him. I'm thinking "okay," coach is going to make Chuck apologize, "beep-beep" wrong thought. Taking us to the balcony, if you walk down the first flight of stairs; you are at an opening, basically outside, if you step down; however, taking the next flight of stairs to the left, you are still in the building, of other class rooms. Coach told Chuck, that he was going to paddle him for, "out-of-name" calling. In the corner was a big red ball, handing Chuck the ball and instructing him not to drop it. Coach hit Chuck, five hard licks, Chuck is crying and is up, on his tip toes but he takes it. Then, coach tell Chuck, to give me the ball. What? Coach, tells me it is because, he had overheard me telling my sister about the incident and went on to say, junior high business is junior high business. Evon is my sister and I can tell her what, I please and furthermore, you should have talked to Chuck and I at that very moment. Coach, was not hearing none of that, he kept insisting, I take the ball. I did not want that ball, especially, after seeing Chuck's paddling and I could not understand, why, I should be paddled. Finally, I held the ball, coach hit me one time and I threw, that ball off the balcony, the ball was rolling toward, the embankment, he instructed me to go get the ball; no I will not go get it and you are not going to hit me again. Coach, was furious at me and suggested, we go to the principle office and I was all in, for that, we walked as far as the high school door; all he had to do was open it, he changed his mind because, he knew, he was wrong and I would have told the principle everything. Twenty- five years later my daughter, Mallari tells me "mama coach Watson do not like you." That's okay with me, regardless of, being opinionated or self-willed, the fact remains, "truth is." A few years later, I saw coach Watson at Bengals, wide-receiver, Carl Pickens' wedding and remember what my daughter, had said to me, so I slipped back into a child's mine as if I need his approvable. I walked up to coach Watson, as a woman, talking as a woman; yet, feeling like a child. He, gave me a crooked smile and a simply hello. I am; now, over it because, I know what it is, he needs to stop looking at me, the child and look at himself, as the teacher, as the man.

For, me every dark tunnel of pain, there is a bright-light of joy and peace around, the next corner. My very last day, in the junior high building, was like a fairy-tale, with the happiest ending every. The last class, I had at the end of the day, was study- hall and I never studied nothing, as for as school work. The teacher, was Mr. Charles Smith, he was one of the sweetest men, I every known. However, he could be hard if need be, I seen it with others but never toward me. Mr. Smith put me in the mine of the Pillsbury doughboy; yes, he was a bit on the heavy side and wore glasses and was funny. Saying, I am going to go get me a drink of water, he would say, "rinse out your mouth and bring me some." One day I did, my mouth was full of water, motion for him to open his mouth to get his water, he laughed and turning red. In this class were eight students, one white girl, my friend Teresa Jackson, whom I stay friends with over the years, sharing much, until she was overcome with cancer, rest in peace my friend. Also, in the class was six white boys, whom everyday place chess against, Mr. Smith and each other, they had some type of bragging rights thing going on. I was the eighth student. Mr. Smith and this boy named Gary were the best. I would stand there and watch them play and ask question and go talk with Teresa some. I started understanding the game and the strategies of their movements. Then, finally got up enough nerves, to sit down and play, I loss; that, was okay, I kept on trying. Then, it happened, I beat Mr. Smith, I had Him in Checkmate, game over, last day of school. Mr. Smith, reared back in his chair, pulling off his glass and tears were literally, running down his face. I became frightened, thinking he was having a heart attack and calling out his name and asking him was, he okay. Sitting back up straight, in his chair, wiping, the tears from his eyes, replacing his glasses, back, on his face and then, he said to me, "tears of joy, the student beats the teacher." We, laughed and gave each other a big hug. I loved him.

My summer was great; playing in the community youth softball league, participating in church activity, camping, sleep over, at my white and black friends' homes. As mention before, first summer job and at summer end; I had saved enough money to buy my own clothes and school supplies. Grateful, to have been able to take; that, burdening off, of my mama. Entering high school, I had high hopes, for the good. The hope of good grades, getting along with, the staffs and students. Looking forward in participating in school activities and sports. My hopes came to pass; for, the good, my freshmen year. My second summer. I did the same things as the previous summer.

Another summer ends and another school year begins. As a sophomore, I had a totally new self- imagine of myself. I knew, I was pretty, dark and lovely skin and an, (36-23-37) body to match. Grasping with the thoughts of toning my behaviors down; by, letting un-normal things slide, talking lower, walking slower and practicing to be meeker. Being choosing my coach Terry Postell to be on the, "Golden-M Girls Team;" which, was perfect timing; for, what I needed for my, "new Imagine." We were uniformed in school colors, black and gold, duties were selling programs, working in the snack bar, backing the cheerleaders up with, battle-chants, serving the football players and coaches, refreshments after home games. After football season ended, the basketball season begin and now, my meekness stood a test.

I had been playing basketball since fifth grade, under three different coaches and to get cut-off the team my sophomore year; that hurt lasted for years. Coach Karen Watson, would had been, my fourth coach; however, she chooses to cut me, from the team and yes; she is the sister of the junior high coach Watson. I asked, the coach why? Also, saying to her, you know, the five freshmen you choose over me, one may have some different better skill then I, two are my equal and two I can beat one-on-one any day of the week. Coach gave me this lame reason; she said, "these five freshmen, I can teach and trained them; for four years and they, can be state champions, their senior year." Seriously"? What about me now, coach decision was made and that's the end of that story. I went to one basketball game to see my friends; that I had been playing with over the years; like Renee, Annette, two other Mary's and the others. I was so sad watching my friends play; I never went to another games. Now, if the coach decision or wishful thinking, had turned out to have, this "great team their senior year." The hurt would have left my soul much sooner. I would have been pleased; to have being the sacrificial lamb.

That did not happen, not only did they not win a championship, they were not good at all.

I made it thru, the school year, summer began and this particular summer was full of summer fun.

Again, working in the summer program, the community as a whole seemed to be, on one accord. Supporting the men's softball league; traveling where every they went. There was social gathering, fish fry, talent shows and camp outs. The church choir was busy singing throughout the county and other cities in North Carolina, Georgia and Tennessee. Near summer end, I began to think about my future plans. Knowing, mama could not afford to send me to college, I contemplate on joining the army, for my schooling to become a doctor. My mother loved the idea and was supportive and encouraging, of the thought. Upon, entering my junior year, I was still a Golden-M-Girl; still on the school's volleyball team; an overall good player, specializing in sever and spiker; I loved volleyball too. However; this lovely summer, was actual the quite before the storm; buckle up your seatbelts; we are going on a painful journey, difficult to remember and even harder to write; of all the stories, this is the most dreaded truth of all; however, if I'm going to tell my story, this one is a must. I accept all the responsibility; for this mistake; yet, there were reasonable, negative incentives; such as, built up resentments, peer-pressure, young, dumb and foolishness.

I think, within five months, of the new school year; I knew the dream was over. Renee and I was at the Friday night football game. We saw her boyfriend, Scott with a girl name, Teresa in the car with him. Renee was in a search for Scott all that weekend, he is nowhere to be founded. Renee convinced me to be with her as she confronted, the girl at school Monday morning. During the confrontation, Teresa and I started fighting, other students watch, while others tried to break us up with no avail. Staff came and pulled us apart, Teresa broke free and sucker punched me and I could not get back to her at that moment. They had Teresa in the principle office, sitting in a chair. As I walked, that way my friend, Charlene, (Sankey) had my purse. I reach inside of the purse and pulled out a knife. Sankey tried desperately to hold me back unable to do so; I went into the office attempted to stab the girl, when my friend Eric, a six-foot, two- hundred pounds football player; picked my five-four, hundred- ten pounds up and flipped me over his shoulder, slapped me across the butts and carried me away. After, the girl was no longer in the principal's office; Eric still with me; went into the office too. The principal informed me his duty was to call the police. My response was given me the phone, I will call them for you; demented. However; I am so, thankful; that the principal selected to have me taken home. After being home along for several hours; my mind came back to soundness. Later on, that evening, the school called; to tell my mother of the event and that, they would be sitting-up a conference meeting for us; I then, had to explain; how, I got caught-up in such mess. My mother cried. Then she said; "I hope this will teach you not to get involved in someone else battle; you see you will fall and they will be still standing." She went on to say, "I do not know what, I can do about this, but you are going to finish your education." Needless to say, that was a long night for the both of us. For me, the realization, I had hurt my mother and myself again. Knowing my mother, she cried half the night and prayed all night.

Several days had past, when we were informed, to come to, the school for the conference meeting. The principal was sympathetic and was sorry about it all; he also expressed; that, he like me, that I was really a good child. He wants me to finish school too; just not there, such behavior is unacceptable and to make sure other students understand that. The school suggested to my mother to send me to family elsewhere and that they would send all my record; without mention, this incident. Her prayers were answered and I learned, the lesson of getting involved in others problems. This is when, I moved to Atlanta; to live with my sister, Irma Jean.

Arriving in Atlanta talking about a culture shock. No dirty roads, buildings taller, then trees; on every corner a bank, pawn shops, restaurants, night clubs, taxis, cars, buses and polices. The sounds of constant sirens; all the bright lights of billboard signs, clothing stores and never had I seen so many "Black people," on every corner; nor driving Mercedes, sporting three-piece suit; the women in elegance dress and the appearance of class. Truly, I am in a new world. The school I attended was West Fulton High School. The school had fifteen-hundred high school students, the majority were Black and so was the staff. Now, I am taking classes, that was not offered at Murphy, such as Black History and dance, modern, tap and jazz. Since I entered during mid-term, I was unable; to partake in most, of the school's activities. However, the students were receptive of me, the boys calling me, "Miss North Carolina and the girl, thought I talked, "proper" and they called me the, "Black White Girl."

Anyways; I carried my mother's tears with me. I had promised her not to disappoint her this round. Staying focus on right choice; no, fighting, be humbling to the teachers, choosing new friends carefully, avoiding the police and no, pregnancy. I finish my junior year without incident. Although, this one girl tried to pick a fight with me in the busy full hall one day; she accused me, of bumping into her but she bumped into me, a few words where past, then the coach, my history teacher, stop the disturbance. I was glad about it because, she had no idea, who she was messing with, I did not want to fight; however, I did not want to get beat up either. The truth is, I was always in this warfare between two full souls of good and evil; either could win at any giving; yet, God's grace and mercy would shine on me in spite of me. As I had mention in my "preface," of my book, I had talked about how God would put the right people in place at the right time to help me. I believe that; how, else can I explain the principal action on my behave and my home-boy, Ford was living in Atlanta with his brother.

Ford had finished school, the year before and to have him there was truly a blessing. Knowing his way around the city; fairly well was good and we spent a lot of time together. Ford's brother, Michael being in the right place at the right time; had started driving the band, "Brick" to their show than became their stage manager, then production manager. Ford and I would go to watch the band rehearse. After that Michael took off; working with Luther Vandross, Run-DMC, Fat Boys, Alicia Keys and Destiny's Child and other singers. Michael's son Jermaine Dupri grew up in the music business; at this time; however, Jermaine was just a little boy and I was his babysitter, while his mother, Tina worked; for Budget Rental Cars. She and I shared a friendship, sharing many thoughts and conversations.

Ford had a yellow Volkswagen, that's how, we got around. One day he had come to pick me up and it was raining a dangerous down pour. He is driving fast, I kept telling him to slow down. As we were coming off a ramp merging into traffic; hitting a water puddle; we hydroplane, the car is spinning on the highway, cars or dodging us and the car trunk is in the front, the hood pops up, the spare tire is suspended and is bouncing across the highway. I got into the floor and I could see us both back in Murphy at Ivies Funeral Home, people are crying and saying, "oh how sad is this." Then the car stops, I am dead or what? The car had stopped; off side of the road, pointed in the right direction and Ford went to retrieve, tire. God is good. When we got to Michael's, I started telling him all about it, Ford was trying to get me to shut up. Heck no; your stupid butt almost killed us. Michael chewed him out.

I returned to murphy for the summer and work again on the youth program. Summer ended and I returned to Atlanta back at the Grants' and this is my last year of school, I got me a job at a restaurant owned by a Chinese man but the restaurant was not Chinese food. I'm good and at peace for about four months, then I became unhappy, missing my mama, Evon and Murphy. The Grants' were good to me; however, like many families; they too, had they're on dysfunctions. I have had enough of Atlanta. I called my mother in tears asking her if I could come home. Assuring her I would attend the community college, to get my GED and enroll into the community college. My mother said okay, come home. I immediately started, to get my house in order, telling the Grants', the school and my employer. A couple of weeks had past, my last night in Atlanta; I had handed washed my work uniforms, scrubbing the bottom pants hems, the next morning, I pressed the uniforms and folded them neatly and placed them in a bag. I went to the my work place, to get my check; the owner/boss was having breakfast with other business men. I approach them, humbly and saying, "I'm sorry for disturbing your breakfast, I have come to get my check." Handing the boss, the uniforms. This man opened the bag pulling out the uniforms, inspecting them; then he made a comment about the bottom hems and that, I needed to but the uniforms into the dry cleaners. I asked this man was he crazy? Saying to him; I'm returning them back, better than, I had received them and the slight visible oil stains are from your nasty kitchen floor; I only wear these in here. He then placed them back into the bag and said, "take them to the cleaners." No, I have a bus to catch, this evening, my mama is expecting me and I'm going home. "No check," he said. I took the uniforms out of the bag; throw them on the table; knocking over coffee, juice, pancakes, bacon and eggs; then I told him he was next, if he did not go get my check. He stood up; shaking like a scared rat and went to get my check. You see, I tell this story because all of this was unnecessary; he chose to dis me and to front on me, in front of his friends; being hard and selfish; not hearing a words of mind; not even caring and this is; not, to say what I did was right, but saying; people gets tired of begin oppresses and denied their; by people in power.

After receiving my GED, I attended Tri-County Community College for about two years. I was certified as an Emergency Medical Technician; for the state of North Carolina. I entered into the school's beauty pageant, winning first runner-up; I received a dozen of red roses and a scholarship, that payed for my, schooling for one year. While attending Tri-County, I began taking English and literature classes; then I started writing articles for the school newspaper, the "Road-Runner Review, later I was writing articles; in the local newspaper; the "Cherokee Scout." My articles, consisted of Black History and community news, each community, had their own writer. I have much admiration for what, I have accomplished through Tri-County; which does not end here, I have two more interval's at Tri-County, that we will come back to later.

At this point, it is the time to really talk about God's; mercy, faithfulness, his *love* and his protection over me. Yes; it is still about begin allowed to make your own choices; however, when you make the wrong choice; if you are already one of His's chosen ones, you are still covered, God covered me with His' mercy until; I could catch up with His' grace. Another way of saying; you make fall and skin your knees but you will get up; also, a way of saying, the Devil is trying to kill us. I am not calling anyone a Devil, but the unclean and unseen spirits, (1' 1 Peter 5:8) that wants to destroy us. As you have read, thus far about my life; all of that is the minor leagues. If it had not; been, for the Lord on my side, I would be dead or spending the rest of my life in prison; He has been good to me. I have said all of this as an introduction into my marriage.

THE MARRIAGE AND
THE CHILDREN

I MARRIED MY ex-husband, Larry in December, 1979, we had known each other since childhood and were, secret *lovers* to many, of the community. We were married, by the Reverend Harvey Kincaid; at his home; that, he shared with his wife, Mrs. Sadie Mae Kincaid; one of mama's friends. Our witness were Larry's cousin Ray and my friend Sara. The pastor said to me, (Corinthians 6:14) Mary I know you are a believer, this man that you are marrying; I do not remember seeing him in church. Again, young, dumb and "in love," I did not listen; nor did I understand what the pastor was saying to me. Which was; "do not be yoked together with unbeliever." How right he was. I jokingly tell people, we were married for twelve years and divided; that, by three; he beat me up, the first four years, I beat him up, the second four years and the last four years; no, one bothers the other one. What away to have lived. However; for me, him being a whore was worst, then the physical abuse. No; respect for me nor, ours sacred bed. I went to my mother one day about, him being such a whore and telling her; that I try to keep him busy and I like it and he response as if he like it too. She told me; that what he does do not have anything to do with me; some men are just naturally whores, he will never stop; also, he will never leave you; so, you deal with it are *leave* him. Before, I get any further about my marriage let me say these three things. First of all, let me say, Larry was raised by his sister a teenager herself, with a drinking man and babies of her and doing the best, she could for him and dealing with a man. In the community at that time many married men were drinker, whores, wife beaters, conceived children from other women and some married were doing the same; common behaviors and pretty much accepted. That is what we saw and what he learned; he did not know how to be a husband. Secondly, after, we had been apart for, four years, he called me wanted to talk; my mind went to, "I hope, he not going to ask about reconciliation; that's a no!" He wanted to apologize; for all the wrongs, he had done to me, asking for, forgiveness and saying, I had been a good wife, to him. Third, I will say, I still love my ex-husband; not the way a woman is; when she is, in love with a man. It is the kind of love, remembering a childhood friend; the kind of love, for the father of our children and grandchildren; the kind of love for a human-being, as God's requested; to forgive and love everybody, in spite of.

I know, by now you are wondering; why would you stay, so long? The number one reason is the, promise "till death do us part," the fantasy of staying together; so that our children would be raised in a two-parent home and the illusion, he would change. Secondly, finances; he had a good job, working for the federal government, TVA, which spans in many directions; such as energy, nuclear, water dams' and recreational parks and he was in a credit union. We were buying savings bonds, had medical Insurance, a three hundred thousand dollars, life Insurance policy, an accidental death the policy, was eight hundred thousand. We were buying a house; we kept two cars, a truck, I had nice clothes and furniture's. A lot to leave behind. Then one day, I looked across the room at him and in that moment; I thought, you have treated me, so badly; that, not only do I not love you anymore, I really do not even like you. Then, my mind went to, I'm tried; you can have all of this, "shit," I just want to be free. Let's start with, two of the whore stories but understand, there were more; that, I caught him at, others I suspected and others I learned about after, I had left him.

One day, he had left the house, with his cousin Ray; they were being to sneaky, whispering to much; for my comfort, until I got suspicious, dummies. I did not know, what they were up to but I knew it was no good. I just let them go not saying a word. After about an hour, I decided to go on a seek and find. I was at a stop; which was a "T" intersection, this car is coming, no signal, on the road; that, I will be getting on. Apparently, they recognized me and stopped in the middle of the road. The mere fact; that, I was already on a "seek and fine," my thoughts were far from a courteous driver, I stayed at the stop sign.

The driver then passed by; I recognize Ray as the front seat passenger, so I follow them. The driver started to speed up, so did I. The closer I got the faster she drove, then I remembered the approaching bridge; I thought if I bump them at the bridge, they would jump the rails and go into the river. I tried. However, she wrestled with the car steering wheel and made it off the bridge. They then pulled off the road near county's dumpers, I pulled in front of them; as I got out of the car, the driver changed the gear into reverse. I got back into my car, put the car in reverse and rammed them; now they are on two back wheels and one front wheel. I go to Ray's side, with a bat in hand, he cracks the window, I ask him where is Larry? He did not know. I took the bat, one hard swing shattering the window. Then Larry came out of the back seat so fast and was on me, taking the bat. I ran into the woods. In my life, I have learned there is a time, to be quiet, to speak up, to fight and to run; not a shame, I have had to do them all. While I was chilling in the woods; they got the cars unstuck; Larry called out for me, I ignore him. He left. I made-up a story to this lady and she drove me to Texana. Larry paid to have my car fixed and the other car as well, the car belonged to someone else, other than that; the other car would not had been fixed. Wild, yes!

My daughter was probably around ten months old; Larry was leaving to go to work. I asked him not to be late, we were running low on kerosene; for our heaters. He is normally home around 5 O'clock. No; Larry a 7 O'clock and the heater flames are getting lower. I wrap up the baby, put the kerosene jugs in the trunk, of the car; then fasten her into her car seat, going to get the kerosene. As I was coming down the road, I see his car at the end of a dirt road, he had stop because a car was coming; I was the driver of that car. Behind him was another a woman; that I had knew, was suspect. I stop stay in the road, he turned left, she turned right and, I chased her. At the stop sign she went straight and I turned left. I had my baby in the car, with me and when I got home, I called and told her husband, the fool did not believe me. And yes, they're more to that story end, I just do not want to keep thinking about that mess.

As for as all the physical violence goes; I'm not going to go into completely word by word stories.

What I will do is mostly summarize; in shorter forms. I do not want to talk, in detail about the time, he attached me and while in the floor my head was probably; the bullet width from the wall and that is where the bullet, entered into the floor; nor when, he held a knife on me while, I cleaned up my own blood off the walls. Nor; do I want to talk about, the time, he accused me falsely at a party, then drove me down to the river, to drowned me; socking me in my face as he drove. When we arrived at the river, he took the keys out of the truck ignition and got out of the truck. I locked the door; continually going from side to side holding the locks down. The police happened to come by cruising, I jumped out of the truck, flagging them down, they took him to jail, I got the keys and went home. Larry was so moody, he would come home many times and

MARY & A-HALF

not, even speak to me, but if my brother, Jerry and his brother-in law, Ray; yes, Larry's cousin would past our house walking to Jerry's house, Larry was all smiles and had plenty of conversations for them. Although, it was I who, had cleaned the house, washed the clothes, cooked his dinner, and went to handle his business. Then, I figured out how he was winning the physical battle. If he was being moody, he was already mad; therefore, I'm already behind. So; since, he came home at 5 O'clock, I started getting mad at 4:45. Then it went like this, I did not speak, nor did he. Later, he would ask, "what is wrong with you,"? Then, I would ask, "what is wrong with you"? If he said nothing was wrong, with him; then I would say nothing was wrong, with me. If he said something threaten, then I would ask him; "what did he want to do?" That's the moment I started winning. Again, God is good; when Larry was being driven, by Satan's demons and trying to kill me, God protected me from death. When, I allowed Satan and his demons to rule over me; God protected us both. He spared, Larry his life and protected me from life in prison or the electric chair. Hallelujah! I shot at him, I chased him with my car, while he ran up the bank for protection and I was riding sideways on the bank to hit him. I stabbed him with an ice-pie, a pair of scissors and cut him with a knife. I hit him, with a lamp; with my little girl's wooden rocking chair and knock him out with a cast iron frying pan. I even cooked him a pot of grits; not to eat but throw on him; I wanted the grits to glue to him.

All of these horrific scenes, I did leave many times; then returned. I had him locked up many times but never was I locked up. I even had to take my children to a battered women shelter. How did I finally escape? As I began my escape plans; I first bought me a pearl pink handle.25 clip pistol. I know longer have the gun. I needed a particular type of Judge; for what I need and wanted. Murphy did not have this judge. I had to drive all most and hour to Bryson-City North Carolina, were the judge was. When Larry left that morning, I left too. I had with me stacks of police reports, medical bills and papers from the shelter. As I talked to the judge; he looking at the paper and I had told him, that I was afraid; I had bought a pistol because, Larry is not going to except this. Then the judge asked me; Mrs. Wilson where is the pistol? Oh, my goodness! I just look at him like a deer in a headlight; unable to speak, so he asked again. I whispered softly, "it is in My purse." I just knew, I was going to jail, sitting in, the judge's chamber armed with a pistol. The judge leaned up, looked unswervingly into my eyes and said; "I am going to give you what you have asked for; I am ordering your county's sheriff department to escort you to your home, you go there; not home and I am giving you this restraining order." Then, he said, "this is only a piece of paper it cannot protect you; do you understand, what I cannot say?" "Yes, I do."

I waited at the sheriff office until; they called in more deputies. Asking me, if I was ready. There were two deputies' cars in front of me with two deputies in each car. I am in the middle in my car. Two deputies' cars are behind me, with two deputies in each car. We drove into the driveway; I was told to sit in my car until they ask me to come. After knocking, two deputies went inside, two stood on the porch, one was on the left side of the front yard and the other on the right side. The other two stood side by side near, the bottom step. I went inside, Larry and I caught eye to eye; his eyes spoke, hatred you." I felt so good and safe; as I gather my things, Larry said, "so you going to haul her stuff.? "No, she is driving her own car." Larry said; "no that is my car." The deputy showed, Larry the Judge order; that he had given me that car. My children and I stayed with my mother; for about a month, then, we rented us a house. At this time, I set two rules; one, being it is now us; we are to love and be for each other always. Secondly; if anyone ask you a question about me, tell them to ask me. There was still some drama, sadness, hurt feeling and adjustments. However, the marriage ended separated, in 1991 and divorced in 1996 and I have never married again. We get along now;

I go to see him and our grandson, Anthony when I am at home. We do talk on the phone on occasion, small talk or about our children and grandchildren issues.

I am a mother, of three; I carried two and raised one. My ex and I married in December; five months later in May his five years old son, Damon moved in with us. Children having a child. When Damon was born, my ex was seventeen, his mother was fourteen and I was thirteen. I had been around, the baby since the day, he was born. I even babysit, the baby a few times; while his mother and grandmother went shopping. I am, thinking; when Damon was about one, his parents departed ways and she moved to Cincinnati, with the child. Some four years later; I am with Larry and now we have Damon or let's sa y; I have Damon and Larry had Larry.

The first year was not easy, with Damon. It was all good; for, me to play "mama," as long as I did "mama," things; accept give him a spanking; that was not allowed. I let Larry know; he needed to step up to the plate and tell, his mother to back off. If I am going to be in the mama role it is going; to be all or nothing. If not take Damon to your mother, send him back to his or I will go back to mine. After we got that straight, all was good. I raised Damon from five until, he was seventeen and Larry and I broke up. However; I have never stop being Damon's mother, I love my son and he loves, his mother. Damon has always been, his mother's fairest. We, have had only one painful disagreement and I will hold the blame. I forgot; how, it is when a man loves a woman; I over stepped my boundaries in their situation; however, it is well passed all is good. Larry and I had been married five years before conceiving, Mallari. Not; that, we did not try and seek medical's advice. Damon, had giving me the opportunity; of motherhood, just in case. After having my daughter, nothing changed with Damon and I. Not, only were, we mama and son; we were friends, road warriors and us against the world.

An area called; Hanging Dog had been a tradition; for years, jumping off the bridge. I had done it, in my youth many times. The last time I did, I almost drowned. I do not know, if I was caught up in a whirlpool or what? I was treading the water; to make it back to the top. Finally, I could see the sun light; yet, my head had not come out of the water. I thought, I am going to die. I begin to pray; not for me but for; my mother, I asked God to take care of her and give her strength, to deal with this; then all of a suddenly my head, popped out of the water. Hallelujah! I then, begin to swim to shore; needless, to say I never done that again. Some twelve years later; Damon comes home; he has a wet towel around him and his shorts were wet. Asking, him were had, he been? When, he told me; where, he had been I almost fainted. I could feel that; same fear, all over again, when I almost drowned, jumping off that bridge. Tears began; to formulate in my tear wells, as I told, him about my own experience. I made him promise me; that, he would never do that, again and I believe he did not. Scared straight. Damon, recently married a childhood friend; I hope the best, for them and I will keep them in my prayers.

Finally, I am with child. One of the happiest days of my life. This baby meant everything to me; of all my mother's children, I was the only one, without having a blood child. The baby allowed me the joy; of experiencing, pregnancy, joined my sibling, of having a child, and my mother seeing my baby. When she was born, she looked; so much like, her daddy and his mama, it was scary; to look at him, then look at her and seeing the same face. This was a good time; for us, for a while. This little girl had everything, she needed and what, was not necessarily needed; toys, a child's car, children furniture, clothing and a big bird, she had to have close by at all times. When the time came to take her off the bottle; of course, she is not trying to hear that and her daddy was on her side. I had stop giving it to her. However; one day she brought me her hiding bottle; I thought they were all gone. I took the bottle, filled it up with water and threw it as far as I could in the woods, behind our house. Talking about shell shocked, she was; but she stops crying and she knew, the bottle was gone. When Larry got home, she started saying, to him "baba-baba." He tells her, I do not know where your bottle is. I never said a word. Mallari, grabbed his hand; led him to the back door and pointed to the woods, he looked at me, I looked at him; he then, picked her up and they went looking for the bottle. After about an hour, they came back without the bottle. I told him, I knew you would go searching; that is why, I put the water in the bottle. I threw it far away; the bottle is gone. Okay; now, mama's I did it my way and it worked.

There is an old saying; "that you will pay, for your on raising." I am a living witness to that as a fact.

However, I will support that statement, further down at this point; I will continue to talk about our children when; they were little after the separation. Mallari was five and Channing was three. Larry and I agreed; that we would rotate every other weekend; one of his weekends, the children did not like his company; nor, their daddy anymore. I let them know; I was sorry that, we had broken-up; however, that has nothing to do with, them and I do not want to ever hear you two said; that you do not like your daddy. He loves you guys; he has provided for you and he will continue to do so. I went on to tell them; our break-up, had nothing to do with them; this is about, him and I and he has been a good daddy for you both. Although; that was not exactly true, "spare the rod and spoil the child." Larry, never wanted to spank them; he and I actually had some fights because of me spanking them. I had let Larry know; those are your children to trains and spank; I am not you child; I am Beatrice Dye's child. I have been spanked and you have no right, to try and rule over me.

Before, moving to, Carrollton, Ga in 1993, the courts had given me sole custody and Larry was ordered to pay child support and he was faithful to that. I was working at Wendy's and every six months, I worked seasonal at the Honey Baked Ham Company; in the evening for six months. I enrolled the children in, Mt, Zion elementary school. Channing was having a hard time; in adjusting, he missed his daddy, Murphy and his cousin Devon. I enrolled him in the little league football and Mallari was a cheerleader; hoping that would help Channing; into accepting the move. It never did. After two years; of being there, Channing got sick. He had broken out in a rash all over, his body; I was bathing him in, oatmeal baths, anti-itch-cream and powers; he was not getting better. I took him to see the doctor.

The doctor walked into the room and immediately, asked me what is going on in my home; that my child has, "Shingles." What? Shingles are an acute infection; which is the same virus, that causes chickenpox. Instead, of coming back as chickenpox, it comes back as Shingles, normally in older adults and brought on by stress. Why is he so stressed? I explained the separation, the new move; we had been there two years now; and I had hoped, he was adjusting. No; the doctor suggested, that *I* send Channing back to his comfort zone. I was devastated. However; I surrender, for my child's health and I called Larry; he came and got Channing, that day. That was hard.

Not long after that; we started our divorce procedures. Larry wanted joint custody; I wanted him to pay for the divorce, buy me out of the house and I would agree to joint custody; only if, when they were with him; I would not have to pay child support. We agreed and the divorce was soon finalized.

Channing is with Larry and I have Mallari. We stayed in Georgia, Mallari and I for a total of six years.

Mallari, like me was rebellious stay in trouble at school, in the home and the neighborhood. Like my mama; I talked to her, spanked and punished her; my prayer life was out at this moment. At thirteen, she had gone to spent the summer with her daddy; which was not a new thing; accept her daddy had promised her, the stars and the moon; this round, if she stayed with him. They called to tell me; I did not like it; however, we had joint custody and maybe, she would do better. Within four months, I get a phone call saying, I am going to be a grandmother. I was tickle pink; my thinking it was Damon; no, it was Mallari. I was silent but not shocked. I knew she was liking boys and I had a tight rope on her. Her daddy was blinded and apparently, allowing to much. When I was able to speak; I first said I am glad, she got pregnant in your care, because and my care your family, would never let me live this down.

Now, I personally do not believe in abortions; however, I want them to know, what their options were. let them know, they could abort, give the baby up for adoption or they had a baby. They decided to keep the baby, Anthony. Larry adopted Anthony from Mallari; grandpa is now daddy. Which was a good decision; whereas, as the baby would be, legally protected, for all of Larry's benefits. The baby will be twenty this year; he has had some medical problems; however, he is good and I love him very much.

Mallari is married now, with three, Samiah is thirteen, Camron is ten, Ju'Siya is five and they live in Chattanooga, Tennessee. Before, Mallari got married about five years ago; she was going thru a lot and I moved back to Georgia; for six months, to help her and the children, then I returned back to Cincinnati, Ohio. Again, I say, she seems as if not to remember that.

Mallari and I have always had this love-hate relationship. Starting when I had Channing, she was so jealousy of him and the love; I showed my nieces. I constantly tried to explain, I love you; I am your mama; why, would I love anybody more then you. The older she got the more manipulated. The more I gave her, the more, she thought, she was intitled to. Life lesson, that I learned; as for as me understand my mama's pains and doing better, I was eighteen; Mallari was thirty and she is still; not completely there; however, she is thriving. About four years ago, she decided to blame me for all of her woes. She wanted me know how I damaged her. Okay, I will claim foul; yes, I had to admit, apologize and accept my role. However; I let her know; "if you are smart enough, to see where, I damaged you, then you are smart enough, to fix yourself." I refuse to be held captative; in, yesteryears mess. I remined her; that she is not the only one, that has been thru something. I am saved, washed in the blood, a queen; of the Highest; why, must I worry about, what a mere mortal, think about me and be forced into shame; that, I have already been forgiving, by the Lord. All I can do is pray for her, encourage, answers her questions, at least those; that, needs to be and keep loving her. We do talk, two are three times a week, she keeps me informed, with truth, half-truth, and I know she keep secrets too; however, I try to see them at least; once or twice a year.

When my son, Channing was born; Mallari was three. Learning I was pregnant, with Channing, I was upset. I had the one, child; no more bottle; nor diapers or sleepless nights and I had lost all the baby weight gained. Now, starting all over again. I accept the pregnancy and started preparing, for the new baby. Evon, had a little boy, Devon, he was probably not one yet; Devon, was such a pretty baby, he is now a handsome man. Now; I am hoping my baby is healthy and pretty too and he was; dark- in-lovely, with the prettiest long silk hair; that laid down; on his head. My son still has a good grade of hair and now, a handsome man too. After Channing was born; he would throw-up most of his food; more so then normal. We took him to his Pediatric Doctor; she thought his body would take care of itself. He was not getting better; we returned to the doctor; telling her, the milk is being; so, forcefully expelled; that the milk is coming out of his nose. The doctor, then made us appointment to see a Specialist in Pediatric in; Chattanooga Tennessee. The doctor, diagnosis was called; Pediatric Gastroesophageal Reflux. Once the food is in the stomach, it backs up into the esophagus causing vomiting. The Specialist explained, this was common in infancy. He wanted to try a treatment of managements. Changing the baby formula, adding a small amount of cereal for weight, and a special design pillow; so, the baby could sleep up-right. After two-week, the baby is doing the same except, he is getting strangled. They, then sent us to Asheville, North Carolina to a Pediatric Surgeon. We were told; that this would be quick and simple; just a few stiches inside to the narrow tube; going into the stomach and we would go home, the next day. After, the surgery; we left my niece at the hospital and we went to get a room. I came back, went into the baby's room, he was gone; I asked my niece, where is the baby? She was not making sense. As I stepped out into the hall; the doctor and nurse are coming toward me and the doctor is carrying the baby. He opened the baby's blanket and I could see milk, literally running down, the outside of stomach. They have to go back in. What a nightmare. I am scared out of my mind. One surgery changed into two, one overnight turned into nine, five days in intensive care, four of those days he was on a respirator and where there was hole a tube was in it; where there was not a hold, they made one; in his arm and neck. Needless to say; how hard, I prayed, asking God to forgive me for not wanting a new baby.

Telling God, I do want him, please heal my baby. God did it. Channing was in his private room for; four days and oxygen for about two of those days. Finally, he is healed; we went home and I kept an eagle eye on him. Just maybe that is why Mallari, was so jealousy of the new baby. I am so thankful; he is fine ever bit of six feet and two-hundred-plus pounds. Naturally, there were questions to be answered; what happen? The case was forcefully settling, by Larry and a crooked lawyer; not keeping his agreement, with us, I wish, I had known then; what I know now.

When, Channing was little, we had went shopping and Channing saw a pair of black cowboy booths, with white thread designs on them; he had to have them. I tried my best to persuade him on a different pair of shoes; no, not happen. Channing loved those booths. That kid in the hot of summer would have on his booths, a pair of shorts, a tee-shirt and get out his toy lawnmower and cut the grass for hours, really.

I had been and Cincinnati, for several years when Channing came to see me. He was having some problems with his white girlfriend. I encouraged Channing to stay; with me for a while. I was willing to help him get part time job and enrolling him, into one of the state colleges or universities. He seemed to have been on board; with the plans. I came home one night from work and this girl was there with her young son; not Channing but another boy from the community. Needless to say, I was shocked; this young girl drove; from North Carolina to Cincinnati along with a small child. I asked had they eaten and they had; then Channing tells me; they are going to work out their differences and he was returning back to North Carolina; with her. I talked to Channing, trying my best; to convince him, to give himself, the opportunities, we had discussed. Again, "free will" he made his choice and returned with her.

Within a few weeks, of leaving; my son is in serious trouble. I was told; that Channing and the girl; had, had some kind of physical confrontation and the little boy got hurt in this mess. I am thankful the boy *is* okay; now and this was over twelve years ago. Then, there were others, saying the incident happened this way or that way; whatever, happened; my son had to do some time for it. Now; as for me guilt or not, he has served, his time for it; I encourage him to keep his head up and do not worry about, what others say and especially those; on occasions, that; wants to rehash and cause pain. Channing do not need remaining, he can remember, himself after all he lived and served it. When all of this happen, I moved back to North Carolina, to be close to my son; so as, my ex and I could go see him; I was in North Carolina for three years. Channing has a little girl, Lenex and a baby girl, on the way.

When, I was growing up and those before me; had issues and a few; like me were "nuttier- then- a fruit-cake." However; I have notice, this "new generation of millennial" something has happened in the atmosphere; that have changed many, of brainwaves as a total disconnect. I see it in mind, my friends, my family and the youth that I have worked with. This one youth said to me; while we were and a conversation on this matter; she said, "yaw raised us." No; "yaw raised yourselves." Sure, many parents are not the parents of old and many still try to be. However; what has happened is the blind, leading the blind, receiving wrong information and really do not know wrong from right. I knew wrong from right; I chose to do wrong. Most have this attitude of entitlement and cannot work; for being on their phones; not, understanding or care; that they are at work to work. One of my millennial bosses, Adam and I was having, the millennial conversation. This young man was well educated and he was high up; in the corporate ladder, only coming by on occasions. He could stand his ground with me on this conversation; until, saying to him; a smart group should come up with a "millennial test" and if they did you would be more millennial then not. He started laughing, I asked him what was funny? He said there is such a test, he has taken it and his results were, he was a millennial and that is not to said a millennial is a bad thing only; to said most need, to redirected their thinking; of what is wrong to what is right. My two millennials are all of the above and they are not along; however; they have another, thing going; what, I call "selective adultness." I know I am not along with this, depending on the matter; they want the right; to decide, on any giving matter; that, they are an adult or child and a split second.

REJUVENATING THE CENTER

EARLIER, I HAD mention; that, there were two more times, I had some other accomplishment, thru Tri County Community college. Well this is the first one; it had been approximately ten years since; I first attended the college. A Catholic, Nun, Sister Terri Martin, came to Murphy and I am thinking, she was helping some students, at the college. The Sister, had been looking around in the Murphy area; to find a place or causes; to invest, herself and the gift of monies, she had been giving, from her parish. Riding thru Texana, she saw a sturdy but damaged building. The building was the Texana Community Center and she wanted to repair the building. Sister Terri asked school staff, who lives in the Texana Community; that could help her rejuvenate the building; they suggested me. Sister, Terri founded out were, I lived and came to talk; with, me of her ideas, I agreed to help her.

I first made-up a survey and walked door-to-door; of the community members asking simply question. Would you like to see the building repaired? What type of programs would you like to see? What can you do, to help? After, I had gathered the information of the survey, the first phases were started. Calling those that was willing to, gut the building, cut the grass and remove the trash. The community came thru; for the most, mainly the same ones though. The next phases, I seek monies from county and state grants. I solicited Tri-County's electrical class to do the wiring, opened up an account; with a local hardware store, payed the plumbers, community members did the sheet rock and an artist painted pictures of mushrooms, grass, butterflies and birds on the walls. After, we had finished; the work, we did have a grand opening, with the mayor, city council, community members and others; for the ribbon cutting and refreshments. The last phase was formulation a Board of Trustees, tutors, chaperons, play days, art, sports and board games. Sister Terri's Parish connection, sent trucks loads of thing; to use in the building and make a thrift store, in one of the rooms. The building was also rented out for private parties. Used for church programs, summer programs; to fed the be grieved families and celebration of the holidays. The community received an award called the Calico Cat; which is a ceramic cat; with assorted patched colors; that, is set on a wooden plat form. The colored patches represented; the most work done on a community center. We had done the most within a hundred miles, in the Western part of the state of North Carolina.

"How great thy are," I am thankful; that God sent Sister, Terri our way, so grateful for her and I am humbled; for my role in this task. However, all was not good; we never received all the help, we were promised. At every phase I would call the promised helpers; few would show up and those that did; did not stay long. There were many days, starting at 8am ending at midnight; Sister Terri, my two children, were five and three; plus, myself. We ate lunch and dinner at the center. We, are in the deep ocean; we either sink or swim. My babies pushed, push brooms and bagged up trash. Sister, Terri and I cleaned out other rooms and dragged trash bags to the dumpsters; that were above the center. I served as the center's Director; from 1991 until I moved to Carrollton, Georgia in 1993. The building is still good and has being, in uses for twenty-nine years now.

The selected Board of Trustees members, were no better; they only wanted to make rule and regulations and nothing else. The night I resign as the center's director; we had a large gathering of community members and served refreshments. People will normally show up if there is food and a "grapevine" speech. The people did not want to be told, what was said; they wanted, to hear themselves, which was great, for me. I first thanked everybody for coming, Sister Terri for her giving heart and those that, were faithful in service. Then I told the crowd a story; of some farm animals. On this farm was a chicken, goose and a duck. One day the chicken asked the goose and duck to help her plant some wheat. The goose and the duck declined; so, the chicken planted, the wheat herself. When time came to harvest the wheat; the chicken went back to, the duck and goose will you help me; with the harvest, of the wheat; they declined; so, the chicken harvest, the wheat herself. Now; the wheat needed to be milled; the process, of turning the wheat into flour. The chicken returned, to the goose and duck; asking can you help me milled the wheat? The duck and goose declined. The chicken milled, the wheat herself. Returning to the duck and goose let's go to my coop and bake some bread; the duck and goose declined. The chicken baked, the bread herself. Now; the aroma of the bread is all over the farm, then the duck and goose came to the chicken; saying, do you need some help to eat the bread. I left it at that; speech over, small talk with the crowd, ate my food and went home.

At this point it is 1993, when I moved to Carrollton with the children and the new boyfriend; that was also from Carrollton. Although, I had lived in Murphy for thirty-three years; I knew my family, on both sides of my parents. As a child, we would go and have week-end summer visit to Carrollton. Also, starting around ten or eleven; my mother would let me spend a few weeks; in the summer with my real dad's oldest daughter, Betty. Betty was the Candie Lady, she sold candy, drinks, chips and ice-creme cones to the neighborhood children.

Betty had two daughter, Mattie-Pearl and Rebecka; they were a few years apart but both were older than me. I remember one summer, when I was around thirteen and mama came to get me. Betty told my mother; that; I was a good listener; Mary will hear you out but; she is going to do whatever; she wants to do. I am still like that; however, the key is listening; you may have something, I need to hear. "Listen." Anyways, is it not funny how life allows us to catch up? I had other cousins and summer friends, my age; that I played with, went to the pool and ballgames too; when I was fifteen, my two nieces are in their twenties; now I am hanging out with them, during my summer two-week's visit; now that I am a completely grown woman; we really enjoyed our time together. Sadly, all three of them have passed on now. I also reconnect to many childhood, Georgia friends and new friends and I continue to drive the two and a half hours ride to Murphy, often to see my mother and friends. However; I am now, going out on occasions to juke joints, clubs, gambling houses, friends' homes of small gathering and what I was not, doing was going to church. I left God completely out; my fault. Growing up in Murphy, as far as; the youth goes it was common to smoking weed, drinking wine or a daiquiri or two; for many, not all and I was one of the many. These, new people in my life were drinking, hard liquor, smoking weed, snorting cocaine and crystallizing cocaine to smoke. All of this is well out of my league; yet, this is where, I am hanging out. A year later, 1994, I am participating in the madness. Although, I am in the "closet" and still able to function; which is a must, I have two children, working and I had to carry myself; in a way that; my mama would not pick-up somethings is not, right with me. A year later, 1995 my mother passes, Channing is in North Carolina and I am becoming bolder; yet, secretly because I still have Mallari and the boyfriend. (Jimmy)

In, 1996 my niece Tiny had been living in Atlanta, twenty-one years. Over the years, she would come, to Murphy to visit, with her children, at the end Tiny had six children. Also, I would go to Atlanta to see her and the children. We two were two peas in a pot and shared much. Tiny did not do any drugs, but she could drink "Old English Beer," all day long. We were both fighters, survivors, and I cursed but Tiny cursed like a sailor. No matter what; she was for me and me for her; so much love between us. One day, in 1996, out of the blue; she came to Carrollton to see me; with her five years old daughter; they stayed with us, about a week. Two-weeks later, I am and Murphy visiting, when my sister gets a phone call; from Tiny's son; that Tiny is dead. Jesus! Dead at thirty-seven, same age as her mother, my sister died.

Hurting, the whole family, three of the children were at an age to take care of themselves, one went with Tiny's sister, the baby, went with her dad and not sure about the other boy, I think the older children had him; she was buried in Atlanta and the children are all grown, doing fine and still lives in Atlanta. Then, again some years later; I recalled that the Lord had allowed Tiny and me some us time before her death. Two years later my daughter, has gone to live with her dad. A year later my boyfriend and I moved back to Murphy, thinking going back home could help our relationship; it did not. I got sick and moved in with Evon and Zeke along and Jimmy is doing Jimmy; which was okay, with me, I was tried of him; after eight years of togetherness. After, I had gotten better; two of my cousins, from Carrollton came to Murphy, for a week-end visit; when they left, I went with them. I lived with my niece Mattie Pearl; everybody called her Ossie. I worked for her. I kept the house clean, cooked food for her gamblers, did store runs; basically, just hustling. For the first time in my life, I have no, responsibilities. My mother is gone; I do not have to be good anymore. I am divorced, my boyfriend is gone, my children are safe in North Carolina and I am grown. I am free. However; that freedom, took me on an eleven years drug addiction; I lived in three different states and five cities. I had been at my niece's place of living and business; for about a year, I was ready to move on. I had a male friend, some cousins and an aunt in Dayton, Ohio; that is where, I wanted to go. I had gambled with the gamblers;

on occasions, I just used my winning to nurse my cocaine fun, that; was now a habit. However; this particular night, I had a plan; not to get high before are after. My focus was to get the money to leave Carrollton; that night I won nine-hundred and sixty dollars and went to bed. The next morning, I had my cousin to take me, to the greyhound bus station and I bought a one-way ticket to Dayton, Ohio.

In the Jungle Now

When, I arrived in Dayton; I rode the city transit, to one of my cous-in's house. She was the one with; some sense and I could trust; with my money, since I did not have any sense. We then walked to the back side of her house, to see my aunt Catherine-Brown-Ackey. Aunt Cat, was shocked to see me but pleased. My aunt Cat was a tri p. She and my mother were different as night and day. She was like her mother. Aunt Cat was good at fabricating untruths and a bit paranoid. However, she liked and loved me. I stayed with my aunt a few months, until I met this guy, he was a good guy, he liked me more then, I liked him; however, we stayed together for two years. I happened to be downtown one day, at the bus stop, he saw me and got *off* the bus. Asking me my name; then we just started a conversation and he asked me did I want to go into this near-by pub to have a beer, I told him, I do not like beer, then he said well whatever you like, I will buy. Now; that's what I liked; he is going to buy; that was a win-win for me. Good conversation, he offered to cook me dinner at his apartment. Asking him where did, he live, he pointed to this nice, seven story building on the corner of downtown; eye distance where; we had met. I asked him which floor, he lived on; he said the seventh. Okay; let me say this; you want to cook for me; if I go and you start acting crazy; I will throw you out the window. He laughed. I was serious. It was a pleasant evening; he invites me back and the rest is history. This man was a cook for a nice restaurant, he also worked on Saturday for a downtown vendor and on Sunday or his day off; at the restaurant, he did the maintenance in, the building. A hard worker, enabler, book smart, common sense average and streets smarts none.

In this secure building; the first floor, was the owner office, accountant office, lawyer office and the outside basement was a jeweler. The second thru the seventh floors were four apartments per-floor; on the roof was used as a patio and the owner's apartment was beside ours. After being there for a couple of months, the owner a wealth white man, begin to say little flirted things to me. I would just smile and kept it going. However, one day I decided, I would call him out on his game. As I was leaving one day, he was in his office; the door was opened like always. He spoke, saying something; so, I asked him; what's up with you? Do you have a jungle fever fetish or do you think, I will swing on a chandelier, for you? He liked that. His response was ooh-baby. Okay, well this is how I see you; as a walking checkbook. It was all understood; we had this connection for two- years too and no; I never swung on the chandelier but, we took care of each other. Yes; I was wrong; I was living my sinners' life; however, I was still being protected and provided for and thankful; for them both. I was in Dayton from 2001-2003.

I went to the jungle, when I wanted to get high. I went probably every couple of weeks and stayed gone for; two or three days. Another, cousins of mind, were on my same page and we did what; we did together. Although, it was not long that, I met and hung out with others addict; then the claws and games started. Again, if you are not; choosing to do the right things and place yourself; with the wrong crowd; you must know trouble will come your way. I knew I was in a dangerous world because that's what drugs are, danger. I had now been doing "coke' for seven years. In North Carolina later; after being introduced to it; in, Carrolton, Atlanta; now Dayton and I thought, I knew somethings but Dayton was a new world of crazies. I stayed true to myself as for as not taking advantage of other and playing the games fairly. I was the one in the hundredth. These crazy people would ask for, a light and keep the lighter or give you the same shape and color lighter but it would be empty. Ask for a cigarette and keep the pack. Give them money on half of the merchandise and they would not come back. Show you something; then give you something else. The real crazies would try to force you into buying what you did not want. You learn quickly if you are going to be in the jungle; you must, shows your jungle side or hang out with certain people; that has, had a good repour with me. Then others took my sweetness as a weakness until I let them know. I had several confrontations and I was; so, mean and serious; that they were afraid and plunked down; which was good for all.

This one guy, I use to go and chill out with a lot, when I arrived, I always had my on package, wine bottle; I would bring him a forty ounce of beer and of course share the pack. That way no games, no confusions nor any craziness. He had never said anything to me out of the way nor showed, he had any crazy fantasies. This day, I sat in my normal chair, by the door; another guy was there on the sofa. Then; the house man reached up above the door and pulled down, this small ax. He tried to give it to me; I asked, what is that for? He said if you do not give us some of your good-girl, you will need this to get out of the house. I looked at him and laughed; then I told him, he needed to, keep it for himself because; for me everything in this room is a weapon. That pair of scissors; on that end table; that thick glass ashtray; on your coffee table; that record rack against the wall and your dead mama's ashes; that are in the vase. He laughs; said I was crazy; hung the ax back up and sit down beside his friend.

This one drug boy; I use to deal with, one day he told me that;

he had been hearing, that I was not; no joke. (mean) I heard you kept a knife up in your bra and you can open it with one hand. (my pops trick) I told him; man, I do not have time for all of this talk; he asked are you going to pull it out on me? No!

Good, you see all my boys with me; they will take you out. I said F-k all yaw. Yaw, should win; you are many, men and I am one small woman. However, they will know who did it, because tomorrow one of you, nose will be in my stomach, one of you, eyes will be yanked out of socked and one of you, lip will be under my tongue. They all laughed and he said you are crazy. Let that be your answers; we made our transaction and I went own my way. So much craziness in danger, seen and unseen, God saw the unseen and brought me thru. You had to watch every movement, hear every word and stay tuned in to your six sense. Let's talk about the; "six sense" we all have; you made not be intoned to it, but nevertheless it's there.

There were times in my addition; that, I knew something was not right; when, I ignore it things, did not turn out good; but I made it thru. Therefore, I learned to listen. Once I was at this house; all was good, a crowd but no drama. Then, all of a sudden, I got this sense something, was not right. I gather up my things; to leave someone asked; What's up; where are you going? I do not know; I am feeling something, I am getting out of here. They laugh and ask is it the drug? I said nothing, I left. I walked down the driveway, crossed the street, turned left, walking up the side walk. Not facing the lights, but I could see them; I turned around and that house was surround; with police, I kept it moving.

Another, time late morning, busses not running so I am walking home; which is, on the other side of town. I knew of this short cut; I was going to take. This time I think it was God. I felt this sense not; to go that way, I tried to ignore the sense and kept moving, the same way. Then it was if, my feet would not move; my heart started beating erratic; then I said "okay God I hear you." At that moment my feet moved; my heart slow down and I walked comfortable, the long way home. Now; I do not know what was waiting; on me, but God did.

Death all around me. I had a friend that had a garage and I was there a lot. One early day I showed up and crime scene tape was around the garage; he had been shot dead. Another girl I did not know but knew of; stole some dope boys' drugs and they beat her to death. A young boy in the game was tied up; with others shot to death executed style. A friend of mind got killed in a car wreck. The thing it is about drugs the means are always the same. It does not matter if you user are sales; the means are the same jails, institutions or death. I did the jail, rehabilitation institutionalize, but God protected me from death.

When my brother Jerry passed and I went home; I knew I was ready to leave Dayton. On my way back to Dayton; while the bus was on a lay-over in Atlanta, I decide to stayed in at Atlanta, for a while; After all I did have connection there. My man, my friend and my sister were looking for me; I had been expected back in Dayton, two-weeks back; now I realize that my selfish self-worried them, they did not deserve that; not knowing if I was dead or not. I first called my sister; she informed me my friends were too, worried. I told her, I would call them and I did; I called them all once a week, I stay in Atlanta for another month; then returned to Dayton. I stayed In Dayton; for about two weeks; said my good-byes, gather my things and moved to Atlanta.

Atlanta most of the same things; just a different day and city. I had a new boyfriend; he was on my whole page. He worked, had his own place, he had common and street sense. He liked what; I liked, I liked what he liked, he was not violent; therefore, I did not have to be. I was crazy about him and he me. Also, I stayed at home; we had the company. Our problem was we were both addicts and we were never going to have anything. Even with that; being said, I stayed from; 2003-2005.

I would walk to the neighborhood store; I did have people that, I went to see and went to purchase, my stuff across the street and there were many, too choose from. However, I only dealt with a few.

Some of them were too cocky for me and would put you down. I was not hearing it. I told many; that they were worst then me. I am sick; why else would, I be in this mess. You want work; you are poisoning, your; on people for profit, and if I get caught; I go to rehab; you go to jail. One night I had walked across the street and this girl, wanted me to go to her man. I told her no. I was not angry with her because, I understood the game; she would receive a pack; for every dollar, she sent that way. As I was leaving, she confronted me talking crazy, I kept walking, she followed. When, we were in the light; I turned around and asked her, what? She was smart mouthing and was waving a knife. I flipped mine, put my chest to her chest and asked her again, what? She looked scared and walked off, good for the both of us. I did not know this girl but, I had seen her. A few days later; we came in contact at the store; she apologizes, explained her game saying; I scared her, she had never been bucked, back and in my eyes, she could see; I meant it. I forgave her and we became friends, I would hang out at times; however, I never had a steady, hanging friend, until her. I often think about her. She had told me about her family, she had been a cheerleader and homecoming queen and her dad wanted her to come home. I hope she has.

One day I was out, my man was at work. I am bored and went walk about. Then "parts" of this song; by McFadden and Whitehead was all in my head; as I walked. The words were as such. "We are going to pull ourselves together; we going to polish up our act now. And if you have ever been held down before, I know that you will refuse to be held down anymore." = "They really do not have anywhere to go; if you ask them where they are going; they do not know." I started saying, God: I know this is you talking to me and I hear you loud and clear and I will get better. I do not like it either, where I am at.

Another day, I was out all day, now it is beginning to get dark and yes, I am a little wired; not high. Guess who shows up again? God! Saying, "I want you to come in." I know you do, but I am not quite ready to do so. I still need you though; to take care of me and protect me from harm; until I do. A few weeks later, I woke up on a Sunday morning; the television was on a gospel channel and they were talking about this book, called the "Book" It was a simplify book of the King James Version; I thought, I need that Book. A couple weeks later, I called my sister to see how she was doing and she asked me did, I want to go to Cincinnati with her; to see our sister Lula-Mae; of course, I did; however, my mind had slipped back to new stomping ground. This was April 2005. When we went, to Cincinnati, I stayed. Same old things; just a different day and different city; Until the blessed day; I got busted buying drugs; that was not mind, getting it for an under-cover, secret users; been there, before; now this date was October, 18th 2005, the last time, I have had any drugs.

The Healing Begins

THIS ONE DAY an undercover police officer drove up on me, fast talking and I could see, he had dope laid out; he asked did I know somewhere, he could get high? I told him I did but first I had to take something to someone up the street; he offered me a ride. I got into the car and, he started asking to many questions and I told him so. I demanded that he pull of the road right now and let me out. He did, I got out and then; these, cops swarmed me like bees. Wow! I started laughing. They search me, got the drugs, my knife and I am still laughing. They asked me who was that; I bought the dope from? I asked him was he crazy? "Snitches gets stitches." Then, I asked; why get me; you should have got him. Still laughing. They wanted to know; if I was high and I was not. They ask me do I need to go to the hospital first? No, why? Normally people, that are being busted and headed to jail, do not laugh. My reply, in a low tone; "that is because you are not police; you are angels in police uniforms; that has come to do for me; what I could not do, for myself and my reigns is over.

I was locked up with a bond, I notified my sister, Evon thru the social service department at the jail; had talked with Mallari and she was getting me out of jail. I told her no. If I leave, I want show up for court, I want to stay; to see what they are going to do, with me. I was locked up for fifty-three days; while there, I was given; by another inmate, the "Book" but God. When I stood before the judge. They had run an intense back ground on me, there were somethings but no felonies. The judge told me, I fit her criteria. Which, was a rehabilitation program. She told me I must finish the program, if not I will be a felony; I will do six months in the state penitentiary; my DNA will be in a data bank and I will owe the state, twenty-five hundred dollars. She told me; she would make these charges vanish, I would be drug free and free to rebuild my life. I agreed.

I was then taken, straight to the rehabilitation building; after the intake, I went to my dorm where, there would be, eventually fifteen of us. Inside the building were two levels and two levels of programs. I was on the top level; the goals were to go home are the bottom level; we were state owned. We were assigned a counselor, three counselor each having five clients. We were expected to participate; with the whole group counseling sessions and one on one with your own counselor. Breakfast was at 7am, lunch at noon, dinner at 6pm, meds at 8pm, snacks at 9pm lights out at 10pm, midnight on week-ends and we all got fat quick. We had two-weeks to turn in your visitor list; of five. I did not make a list. Of that list those were the ones; that had to give you money and buy your supplies. The Director came to see me about my list; I told her I did not have anybody. She knew I had a sister and a niece here; I told her; I was locked up for fifty-three days and not one came to see me and I will not be asking them for nothing. Then, she said what about your sister in North Carolina. No! My sister has her own family and I will not be asking her to do that. She, told me I had better figure out someone. I told her; I will rinse out my dress every-other-day and wash my underwear every night until I leave. She came back the next day with new clothes, underwear, washing powder; body supplies and sleepwear. God is good. We all had the same number five and the same color silver; for random drugs checks. We, were to call the hot line every night. Any time the color silver or the number five showed up together are with another number are color we had to go drop and the house could check you randomly too. We also had to stand before the judge once a month; either she came to us; we met in the cafeteria or taken to the court house; in the county's police van. This was all about our progress. Hard, there were times I had to drop three or four times a week and other times; no drops for two-weeks. I had bus token to go to the outside drop building. If you missed a call and you had a drop, you would be considered dirty and would be locked-up for three days. I never missed. We also had to do three NA or AAA meeting a week. We were all level one the first thirty days; we were only allowed downstairs to eat. Not allowed outside; without a group meeting with the counselor and not allowed to smoke cigarettes period. Depending on your progress; you leveled up to level two; which, allowed two level twos to go downstairs and your family could take you home for a week-end visit. Level three you could go downstairs along and you could escort a level one downstairs and find a job.

Now, there is fifteen women; from all walks of life and you have been allowed; to live and do as you please; without rules and regulations. The purpose is a just cause; however, fifteen addicts are going to bump heads and that was not allowed. You would be taken out of the program, zero tolerance. We did have some blow ups; however, we kept it secret and intervened. The group I was with, were three white registered nurses, two white licensed practical nurses, two black licensed practical nurses and one doctor's white office manager. The others were two blacks from, the streets, three whites from the streets and two whites; that had hidden the truth from there family. The nurses were stealing meds, that were to be thrown away, short cutting their patients, sucking meds off of patches and whatever else. The office manager was stealing the free sample from the pharmaceutical's companies and doctor's office. The rest goes without saying. The nurses and office manager had to humble themselves the most. Not, only did they have the courts to deal with; they had the state board of nurses; loops to crawl thru, if they want their license back. They had to work common jobs, cashiers, cooks, waitress, and in malls. I have learned over the years; the office manager is well; got her job back; two of the registered nurses or well; got their licenses back; one of the licensed practical nurses got her licenses back and other is well working for an assisted living company. I do not know about the others; just me and I am well and full of joy. I did get into a reality check with one of; the nurses during a group session. For what every reason, she thought she was different and was pleased; with herself because, she never was never in the streets. I told her, to look around, do you see where you are at. No; maybe you were not in the street; but if not for this program, you would be in the streets buying; from street pharmacies. I reminded her although; you may have laid in; your bed drinking mixed drinks, wine and taking pills, you stole; from your employer and patients; you are still a drug addict like the rest of us. Maybe worst. She later thanked me for that.

Our group sessions, consisted of several area; such as, role play and chats. These were the moments, of truth and the tears would flow. The remembrances, of hidden pains, hurts and sharing them. Some of; these women had been raped, beating, victimized by incest, punished by going to bed hungry, learning daddy is not daddy, not treated like other siblings and this is just a few. The other group sessions; which represented eighty percent of the program. We had in-depth printed study sheets; however, we were giving a card; with same information, that was highlighted, in shorter form. This card was represented, as our driving license; we had to keep, this card on us every day. All of this information was a publication, of **"Truthought 5 Day Academy Manual." (Copyrights MCMXCVIII Truthought)** The premise of this publication is that; "we do not think right." This represent; not only drug addicts, but people of all walks of life. I also hope; that this premise, will be taught in our school systems. Although, this premise is; too much information; to go thru it all; nor give a lot of examples;

however, I will summarize, the premise. The first one is called; **"Time-Bomb Tactic;"** avoid responsibility and accountability, shift blame or focus, lies and deceives and ignores obligations. Next is **"Thinking Barriers;"** there are nine of them; in the words will speak volumes; closed thinking, victim-role, superior self-image, reckless attitude, instant gratification, fear of losing face, power control, possessive attitude and uniqueness. Last; yet, the most important nine; of all ls, **"corrective thinking."** Choose to be open and receptive to new ideas, be responsible for your own life, know you are capable of both productive and destructive behavior, do whatever it takes to achieve worthwhile goals, use your pass as a learning tool, honestly face fears, admit them; take steps to change them, realize you cannot control every situation; nor control other people, treat others with respect; the result is self-respect; lastly recognize your true value; you are neither greater nor less than others. What a world; if we all changed our actions and thinking; this whole premise, causes my mind to go to; Romans 12:2.

I have been guilt; of the whole premise. However, two of them was, the hardest, to let go. "Fear of losing face," I had created; within me an attitude, of self- pride and viewed fear as a weakness. This behavior manifested into aggression and anger. I thought, I had to keep this; for protection; then I learned to simply avoid nonsense. This is how I live now; however, I realize there may come a time; avoidance, cannot be avoided. I just do not, have to live; "on your march get set ready gone." The other one was, "uniqueness" pretending to myself; that, no one has, been thru like me; unrealistic, we all have been thru something and when you hear about others; you begin to see, you really have not been thru nothing.

The program was set; for you to leave and go home in ninety days; however, you still had to do finish the program. I stayed upstairs for, one-hundred and thirty-three days. Why? I was getting the program although; I had not quite got it. I cannot remember why, I was angry; I just would not talk during group, even when asked. The counselor of the day, wrote my behavior up in a report; therefore, I had to go see, the judge two-weeks early. I had to pack up all my things because normally; you do not return. The day of; the director sent for me; she wanted to know, what are you going to say to the judge? I did not know. She told me, I had better think of something; we have two hours. I told her I will know when, she asks me a question. Okay; she said what if; the judge asks you; what does your recovery mean; to you between one and ten? I will say eleven, she laughs and sends me back to the dorm. The director and I are standing in front of the judge, the judge asks the director, how is she doing? This woman tells the judge; that she is doing great, Your Honor. What? The judge tells me; that is good, your director is pleased. The judge, then asked me; what did I want to said to her. I started crying. When I was able to speak; I told her; I have been angry all my life. This very moment I realize, I can and I must let it go. This woman lied to the judge for me; she saw something in me. God is good.

When I returned to the dorm, the ladies where happy for me; yet, they said you are the director pet; she bought your things, she allowed your sister from North Carolina to see you twice; pass the allowed two weeks period and she had to have convinced the judge. I am blessed and highly favored.

The idea is to send you home. I had nowhere to go. Finally, I went downstairs; which was basically a half-way house. This was good. I had more freedom, allowed to smoke, could go outside and working. Still calling the hot-line and still doing the NA/AAA meetings, I have two new counselors, one is for the new program where, I am living and the other counselor is the same program of the courts except there are group meeting with other clients; in another facility. I was not allowed to cash my work check. The program kept the money to save; for when, they thought, I was well enough to be on my own. If I needed something, I had to put in a request to my counselors. I lived downstairs for seventy- seven days. I was inside a total of eight months and twenty-three day. Jesus! After I moved out, into my new apartment; I did six months of the program same things on the outside. Calling the hot-line, meetings, group sessions, one-on-one with counselors, seeing the judge, working at least the required thirty-two hours a week and I forgot about, our assigned probation officer; we had to see, her in her office on occasion.

I was chained down, forced to follow strict rule; If I want the rewards of the program. I was in captivity; for fourteen months and I needed *it* all. As hard as this program was; I am no longer in the bondage of eleven drug usages. That had taken over me; too the point; that, I had been sober for about six months; standing at a bus stop, when I heard birds singing. I looked for the birds, I realized, I had not heard that sound in eleven years. Why? I was either high or my mind was on; how was I going to get high. When, I finished the program; they, had a graduation from the program; with city leaders and others attending; I was a speaker of three representing, our success. They have a saying; that, "every addict has one relapse in them, but every addict does not have another recovery *in* them." I believe the latter part; you may not recover again. I know I would not. I would be so a shame; of doing something; that God had brought me out of. I would probably commit suicide; *if* the, shock to my body, caused by, the drugs do not kill me first; I cannot and will not; take, another chance on my *life*. Grace, mercy and determination, has kept me drug free, fifteen years, October 18th 2020; so thankful. (2nd Corinthians 4: 7-10)

MARY & A-HALF

Maintaining My Sobriety

As THANKFUL AS I am; for the courts, and the programs; I am happy to be free; from them too. Now, it was my *time* to *live,* recall and play the tapes backwards; to remember, so I could stay free. Time had passed, working, have my own apartment and have founded a Bible teaching, Spiritual filled Church and sober two years at this point. I *will* talk more about my Church later on; however, I will say this; I have known of God all my life; I knew things about Him; yet, I did not know Him; now I know Him and I am in his presence *every* day.

When Channing had his problems; I *moved* back to North Carolina, for three years and I was a bit fearful. I knew I had to stay busy; not to become bored, lonely, angry or tired; that, would have been unhealth for me. My first thing; to, do and my last time at, Tri-County Community College. I worked thru work-study program; in the school's library; I enrolled into the college, in 2008 and finished in 2010; with a Certificate of Medical Transcription, an Associate Degree in Applied Science/General Occupational Technology and recognize, by school officials, as a member of Alpha Beta Gamma Honor Society;

which is a National Business Honor Society; that, requires a cumulative grade point average of 3.0 or higher; be enrolled in a business related program and have earned a minimum of twelve credit hours toward a business-related degree. God is Good. Education was a must for my mama; she would be so proud.

Also, I started, while enrolled in school a **Narcotic Anonymous/ NA** group using the community center *every* Monday night, for three years. The meeting was called, **Healing ON the Hill Group.** We were a legit group; of **NA World** Services out of Van Nuys, California; we were registered with a group code number, region-Carolina and area-North Carolina Mountain.

When I first returned, to Murphy I stayed with Zeke and Evon; for four days and then, I rented mama lse house. After being in Murphy a few weeks; I was visiting Evon. I looked out the window and I saw a friend that; I would get high with. Seeing him took me for a "lul-lul." I mentioned to Evon; that I needed to go home; she had seen, him too. She said to me "girl," do not start. I assured her; I was not; I just need to go home. As I was walking home, I was so afraid and literally trembling. As soon as I opened my door; I pulled off the sofa's throw pillow; unto the floor and begin to pray. I pray to the Lord, of my fears and I told Him, I know you have not; brought me this far, to leave me now. I need this fear and doubt gone. As I prayed, I could feel His presences and I knew I would be fine. I few days later, I saw him again; no effect on me; we spoke and I saw him often during my three years there; no effect on me again. God is good.

Another time Evon, had come to visit me. She saw my daily medication out on the table; she wanted to know; what's that all about? Well, first of all pills were never, my things and if they; had been, she would not have seen them; I would had already taken them. She laughed. My addiction had taken a tow on her too. It took a little while; before her trust was surrendered; now fifteen years in, she has; no doubt. While there, I went to church, worked; went out to dinner, with friends, played Texas's Hold'em, visited friends, and went on, week-end trips.

After my schooling; I started, making planning to return to Cincinnati. I had called my, sister Lula Mae; to see if, I was still going to be able to stay with her. We know how that ended. However, I was saving money, sold all of my large furniture, changed my mail; to a forwarding address, I am ready to go. Leaving was hard; for, my family my closes two friend Gerri, Virginia (Wad) and myself. However, we understood, I needed to be; where, I really wanted to be.

I love Cincinnati. This city has city problems; however, it is where, I got well, plenty to do; with a small-town atmosphere, this city steps-up in crisis. We have toy drives, winter coat drives, walkathons, for many causes, the medical field offers, free health screening and large companies are always giving. My church, New Mission Missionary Baptist Church; Pastor, Tracy Venus, First Lady, Venus and son. The church is a teaching church, we feed the hungry two days a week, different missionary groups, classes, several choirs, praise dance team, participate in charities, youth scholarship program, visit other churches, visited by other churches; just mentioning a few and most of all spirit filled.

After I returned to Cincinnati in 2011; after staying with my niece for four months, I found a rooming house. I had a room; that I had set up like an apartment. I had a walk-in closet, a bed, chair, small refrigerator, a crook pot, electric frying pan, toaster oven and a hot plate. I lived in this place; for four years and I drove the gifted, 1993 Toyota Corolla; for six years. I was grateful; that, I had my own place and thankful, I was not riding the city transit. However, it was getting old to me; I wanted to upgrade; instead it got worse. My car had some problem, I walked to work, a friend picked me up for church, then I got laid off. My, God what is really going on. I was feeling weak a bit depressed and praying. You see I have learned; that, God never promised us; it will always be easy; if I could praise Him, when things were good; I must trust and praise Him, when they are bad and I did.

Then, this happened all in a week time. A sister from the church called me asking, what is wrong with my car? I did not know? Then, she asked, how are you? I have been laid off, but I have applied for unemployment. She later came by my place; with her sister; with a hundred and fifty dollars, she had collected; from, the women book club; that I am a member of. Then she gave me a phone number of another member; that wanted me to call her. I did. The next day she came and took me grocery shopping; telling me, I had a hundred dollars to spend. The next day an usher from the church is an auto mechanic came to fix my car. No charge. The money, that was left from the car part of sixty dollars, were giving to me. The next, I went to check my mail at my post office box and Evon had sent me eighty-five dollars. God is good and He always; shows up for me. If I abide in Him; He will abide in me. If I draw near to Him; He will draw near to me and you too; If you seek Him you will find Him too.

I am thinking it was about six months later; I was asked could I go stay with this lady; the sisters, asked; so, as she would not be put in a nursing home. I did. I stay with her for a year. She had a nice home and I had my own bedroom; rent free. I was also, working for Kroger's. This is when, Mallari was having issues and Kroger's allowed me to go; to help her for a while; staying, for six months and I worked at the Kroger's in Georgia, then transferred back to my same store in Cincinnati. Within two months, I had a one bed room apartment and a 2007, Hyundai Sonata; remember, I wanted to up-grade. Now, I am tired of moving back in forward to Cincinnati; this is my home and where, I am going to stay; until, I wanted to leave. All I have to offer is Jesus and share what; He has done for me; He will do for others; If they sincerely seek Him.

I am not alone here; not only do I have my church family; I was adopted into the Crawford family in 2006. I met the mother first. After begin in her presence, about three or four times; she said to me, "I have six grown children; two yellow boys, (light skin) two black boys (dark skin) and twins' brown girl; what I need is a black girl." I laughed; then I agreed. I have been with this family ever since. I really feel, like a member of the family. We do holidays together, birthday parties, children events, wedding, and pro ball games and anything else families does. We lost our mom, Mrs. Maggie-Lou Crawford in February, 2020. Much love and gratitude; for her, rest with Christ in peace.

There is no way, an impossibility; for me to name all my friends, I have to many. Most has been my friends since; seven or eight, black and white. Now, it is fifty years later and the bonds are the same. I also have new friends; that has, been in my life; for ten to twenty years and the past five. I am afraid to name because, I might leave out one; they know who they are and our personal relationship. I have friends from schools, jobs, church and communities; that are my age, older, younger, men and women. I love you and thank you for your loyalties. You have always loved me as I was and never turned; yours' backs; on me, thru it all God bless you; for that. I will mention one name; my friend, Jenny. Jenny's mother, Miss Grace; my mothers' friends. Jenny and my friendships, has lasted over fifty years. I am one day older, then she. One day Miss. Grace, said to me; "I do not understand; Jenny and your attraction." "Yes; ours backgrounds are different; but we are more alike than not." People tends to misunderstand us; they make-up in their own minds; who, we are; which is farther from the truth.

Jenny, comes from an upper-class family, but she does not; think she is better, than none. Jenny is not violent like me; however, do not get it twisted, she will let you know and show you; if necessary. Jenny, lives her life; her way she will not allow anyone; to control, her decisions. She is free hearty and our love is authentic and lasting.

LET'S GO BACK TO
MURPHY AND TEXANA

IT IS IMPORTANT for me; to say more about where I was raised. We are a town and community; that, had doubt and fears, when Peter Jenkins, author of "Walk Across America" show up in our town; with his dog Cooper, an Alaskan Husky. Some thought he was the FBI, others thinking he was hiding from the police are maybe even a spy. However; I first met him along with others at the ball park. The Oliver brothers, part of the Texana community invited him to go home with them. My understanding, Peter slept outside in his tent for maybe a week, then the Oliver boy's mother insisted, that he sleeps inside.

Peter stay in Murphy; for a while; maybe a year or so; unsure; however, even later joined, by his girlfriend Tina. Peter was comfortable and his surrounding and the community was too. This is the heart of Murphy/Texana.

Although; I finished my high school, schooling; the same year as my class; just not with them. I missed out on nothing, concerning the class. I went to our prom, with my friend Ricky; which is a funny story.

Ricky's girlfriend was from a wealth, white family; he could not take her; however, she picked us up and took us. Ricky and I was long time childhood friends, excellently athlete and all sport. My friend, Ricky, passed away some years ago. I have been invited and attended several class reunions; matter of fact; I just attended ours forty-one years, class reunion in July, 2019. This reunion was most humbling. Many of our classmates has passed on and we, decided to meet again in five years instead of ten. We joked about our conversations, talking about, some having diabetes, high blood pressure, deteriorating, visions and hearing; not pep-rallies, class tests; nor, the future plans Also, most humbling of all was; my high school principal and his wife was there. I finally got up, enough nerves; to go and speak to them. He invited me to sit with them and I did. I brought up; the knife incident; I want to thank him; for what he had did; for me and forgive me for; my behavior. He told me; that, him and his wife had been in the school system for; I think forty years. He understands youth and he was happy to see; me well; as well as, I was to see them well. God is good.

Murphy's population is seventy-nine percent White, nine percent Black and the rest, Hispanics, Asians and American Indians. Why is this information important to me? Back during slavery, it was White, abolitionist; that worked; with the Blacks of the; underground railroad; to help free slaves; to the North. Also, it was Whites; that marched, with Dr. Martin Luther King during the civil rights movement and it was my town of Murphy; that held protests marches, over the death of, George Floyd. I am proud of Murphy. Mr. Floyd death set off these protests all over, the world. Yet, there were others deaths, Eric Garner, Breanna Taylor, Mya hall, Akai Gurley, Anthony Hill, and Sandra Blane; just to mention a small few. Then, in Florida a vigilante, was set free after shooting and killing; seventeen years old, Trayvon Martin. Also, in Georgia Ahmadu Arbery, killed by three white men in February, 2020 has just been indicts and that; is only because the world is looking. As for me; whatever, happens in this case; I know and we; as Black people know; this was pure racism. What these murders seem to; not, understand or care less, these victims; that, they casually kill are human beings. Gods' Creations, flesh and blood, fathers, mothers, brothers, sisters, aunts, uncles, cousins and beloved friends, to somebody. While working at Kroger; when, little white children, speaks to me; so affectionately, I feel sad. My heart feels pain, because my mind wonders; if this child will be taught; to, hate my dark skin. I have many bi-racial children in my family. Not, all of them but many does not; have a relationship with, their white side of the family and that is because; they are not welcome. I wonder who they think they are?

I wonder why; they feel so; much superior? I wonder who died and left them ownership? As human beings; we must not, waiver and the effort of fair justice and stomping out hate; for any race; for all mankind. As for me, being a christian and a "Black" woman; I clearly understand, this evil world. If you do not; look up, any of my suggested scriptures, read this one. (Ephesians 6: 11-18)

UNDERSTANDING
SUMMARIZED HISTORY

ECCLESIASTES 1:9, WHAT has been will be again, what has been, done will be done again; there is nothing new under the sun. Wow! When Egypt wanted to keep the Hebrews as slaves; when Hitter, thought; his race, was most superior, and when white slave owner; said one thing and done another. Understand, the slaves owner's mentality; I do not agree with it; if I had, that mean spirit mentality; I would not want to lose my free labors either; so much so; that, it was one of others reasons; for the American Civil War; of 1861 until 1865. The north wanted to be loyal to the union; however, the south wanted to disaffili-ate from the union and wanted to form confederate states of America. White people; how, have you not understood; that a war; that lasted, amongst us American for; four years and it is settle? No! This has been festering in America since, 1776. I understand why; you cannot see; that's because you have never been Black. Another reason is denying knowing. Racism is in; members; of your families; you just look the other way.

I am sad; for George Floyd family; however, God makes; no, mistake; he was the choosing and suffering sacrifice to make all; of us, stop denying, the truth; which is hate and racism lives. The protests are good and needed. As for as; the violent and the stealing goes; I think most is about; hurt and frustration; however, much is about opportunity; to take and demolish unnecessarily.

I saw this hatred of; Blacks, peek out its ugly head when President Obama was running for president. I saw even more when he won and when; he won the second time even more so. Again, if it had not been for; the support of White people; he would not have won. Whatever it is unite; we stand, divide, we fall.

When, President Trump announced; he was running for president; talking crazy, saying untruths, and his pledged of; "making America great again" for who? It must have been; for those, that; thought, he was Santa Clause. It was like Christmas; for all, the secret haters of racism. The green light; was given; to let it be known; show, yourselves in real likeness. However; no surprise to me; I can see your hate; in your eyes. I can feel your hate thru my spirit; your presence sends out demons; in the atmosphere; that does not match mind. Also, did you know; that, everything about life is in the blood? The same blood. Can you hate my; black skin, so much; that you would allow, your beautiful, long blond hair, baby blue eyes, pretty legs, nicely built, smart and sweet daughter; died, instead of me, giving her; my blood red/black blood?

CORONAVIRUS/COVID-19

WHAT'S THAT ALL about? I do not know. What I do know is Satan; has been trying to kill God's most precious creation; which is mankind; since God threw Satan out of Heaven. What I do know is that; God has been known to send plague, caused lands to be dissolute and famines. When, human-being, forgot about God and doing all sorts of evil. What else I know; is God, is still on the throne and allowing this. God's has all the power. We have forgot and others think; they have the power.

I was curious; in what is in the naming of Coronavirus. Under an electron microscopic examination; the virion (outside of host cell) surrounded by, a "halo" shape. Wow! From astronomy; when gases blanket, the sun and stars; the sun's corona is most visible at the time of a total solar eclipse. The shape is erratically; with a "pearly" radiance. Wow! The anatomy (body) bears the resemblance of a "crown." Jesus! I believe; that everything is preordained; nothing is a coincidence. This virus has shaken the whole world. The thousands of deaths; we wear masks, cannot co-mangle, nor dinning out, nail done, haircuts, shop, entertainments gone, vacations over, churches closed, jobless; just mentioning a short few; of things. Cannot do much of nothing; accept stay in the safety of our homes. Also stop looking at governments to fix; they are, just mere men; this is bigger than, men. However; God is good and he is who; we need to be talking to and keep talking to; when, this is over. It will be; God has intelligent human-being; that, He will guide to solve this; on his time.

Final Words.

THANK YOU; FOR taken interest in my book of life. I make no apology. I have chosen; to allow God to order my steps. Isaiah 55: 11 It is the same with my word. I send it out, and it always produce fruit. It will accomplish all I want it to, and it will prosper everywhere I send it. "God's Promise." Make the Lord keep and bless you all

Mary L. Brown-Wilson